Classic
AmigaOS
Programming

The network

E. Th. van den Oosterkamp

I'd like to take the opportunity to thank the Amiga community for their support and kind messages for my previous books and hope that this one will be found useful as well.

Edwin, Worcester

ISBN: 9798301294907

Web site: www.edsa.uk/amiga

Author: edwin@edsa.uk

Table of Contents

0. Introduction

Back in the day any model of Amiga could be used to connect to the Internet. This happened via a dial-up modem that was connected to the serial port. However, connecting to a local network was mostly the domain of the big-box Amiga models like the 2000, 3000 and 4000. However, with the introduction of the 600 and 1200 models the wedge-shaped systems could also connect to a local network, this time via a network adaptor card in the PCMCIA port.

Today any Amiga can join the local network thanks to devices like the Plipbox and the PiStorm. The availability of devices like these makes Amigas with an Internet connection more common and in turn it makes developing Internet aware applications for AmigaOS considerably more interesting and useful.

This book is aimed at developers who are familiar with programming applications for the classic AmigaOS but have no experience with creating applications that use the network. Most of the examples are in C but there are a couple in 68000 assembly as well.

The first chapter describes where to find the development kits and the compilers and explains how the examples can be natively compiled as well as cross-compiled using a modern OS.

After that this book basically consists of two distinctive parts. The first part deals with IP networking, starting with the basic functionality of a network. From there it gives a detailed overview of the protocols in the IP networking suite, followed by a reference of the most used functions of the socket library. The last two chapters of this part, chapters 5 and 6, show coding examples in C and assembly respectively.

The second part of the book deals with SSL/TLS encryption and the AmiSSL library that provides this functionality on the Amiga. This part starts at chapter 7 and gives a brief explanation of the different algorithm types used by TLS. Chapter 8 is a reference of some of the functions provided by the SSL library and Chapter 9 and 10 show coding examples in C and assembly.

1. Starting development

There are two popular methods for developing Amiga software. The first method was the most popular back in the day and is development done natively on an Amiga. Native development can be done on real hardware but can also be done on emulated Amigas. The second method is cross-compilation where the development is done on a modern OS (Linux, Windows or macOS). Both methods are supported by the C examples in this book.

For native development the C examples have all been tested with the VBCC compiler while using the AmigaOS 3.2 NDK as well as the SDK for AmiSSL. To test them they were all compiled and run on an Amiga 1200 as well as on a Windows 10 PC running WinUAE (version 5.3.0 64-bits). The assembler examples were tested with Asm-Pro and HiSoft DevPac.

For cross-compilation the C examples have been tested with the GCC compiler, also using the AmigaOS 3.2 NDK and the SDK for AmiSSL. After compilation they were tested using the same systems as the natively developed executables.

The Amiga 1200 that was used for testing has the Roadshow IP network stack installed. The WinUAE emulated Amiga has been used in three different test setups. The first setup used the built-in network stack of WinUAE while the second test setup used the Roadshow network stack. The third test setup used an AmigaOS 3.9 installation with its Genesis network stack.

Just like with my previous Amiga programming books all example files are available for download from my website. I also try to make sure that an archive with the most recent version of the examples is available for download from Aminet. I do tend to irregularly update the examples by adding more examples to the archive and fixing problems that may have been found.

The examples for all my books can be downloaded for free at:

https://www.edsa.uk/downloads

Please note that with the source code of the examples clarity and readability of the code is deemed more important than the efficiency of the code. The examples are therefore not meant to necessarily show the most efficient or fastest code or even the best way to create an Amiga program.

Native development

This section will explain where to find the native compiler, the development kit for native Amiga development and the SDK of the SSL library and how to install them on a real or emulated Amiga. Due to the size of the development kits a hard disk is required to make everything fit.

The NDK

The Native Development Kit, or NDK for short, contains all the header files and include files required to develop software for the classic Amiga. Additionally, it also contains the *autodocs*, which document the use of each function for each library and device that is part of the OS. With the release of AmigaOS 3.2 by Hyperion Entertainment a new NDK was released as well. This release has in the mean time seen 4 revisions of which the most recent one can be found at the following location on Aminet:

http://aminet.net/dev/misc/NDK3.2.lha

The lha archive can be unpacked directly into a directory. My preference is to create a directory named *Develop* on my DH1 partition and store all developer related files in there. I have also created an assign in the S:User-Startup for Develop: that points to this directory as follows:

```
assign Develop: DH1:Develop
```

In the Develop directory a directory named NDK_3.2 has been created. Into this NDK_3.2 directory the contents of the lha archive were then unpacked.

AmiSSL

The AmiSSL library is a port of the OpenSSL library and is still actively developed. Each time a new version of the OpenSSL library is released a new version of AmiSSL is released. The latest version can be found on GitHub and downloaded from the following location:

https://github.com/jens-maus/amissl/releases/

There are two files of interest on the releases page. The AmiSSL-x.xx-OS3.lha archive contains the AmiSSL library and the accompanying files for AmigaOS 3.x. These are the files that an end user will need to install in order to use any software that uses SSL/TLS. Installation of these is done via the installer script that is part of the archive.

The second file, AmiSSL-x.xx-SDK.lha, contains the files only a developer will need. This archive does not contain an installer, but its contents can simply be unpacked into the previously made Develop directory. This then creates an AmiSSL directory inside the Develop directory.

The VBCC compiler

When I wrote my first book in 2018/2019 VBCC seemed the only native C compiler for the Amiga that was still actively maintained. Since it still is being maintained (at the time of writing) and is also capable of cross-compiling Amiga software using a Windows system I've seen no reason to switch over to a different native compiler. The two archives required to install the native Amiga version can be downloaded from the following locations:

http://phoenix.owl.de/vbcc/current/vbcc_bin_amigaos68k.lha

http://phoenix.owl.de/vbcc/current/vbcc_target_m68k-amigaos.lha

After downloading, first unpack the bin archive to a temporary location. This will create a vcc_bin_amigaos68k directory, which will contain an install script. When the installer asks for the drawer to install into, select the *Develop* drawer created earlier. The installer will add a couple of assigns to the S:User-Startup file. Before installing the vbcc_target archive it is best to reboot the Amiga to make sure that these assigns are all active before installing the target archive.

The second archive needs to be unpacked to a temporary location as well. This again creates a directory with an installer script. At one point the installer will ask where the NDK has been installed, upon which the Develop:NDK_3.2 directory needs to be selected. This installer will also add a couple of assigns to the S:User-Startup, which again will become active after the system has been rebooted.

Building the examples with VBCC

To build each of the socket library examples the following command is used from the CLI/Shell:

```
vc -lauto -IDevelop:NDK_3.2/SANA+RoadshowTCP-IP/netinclude -o <output> <input>
```

Where the <output> argument is replaced with the name of the executable to be built and the <input> argument is replaced with the name of the source file.

To build each of the SSL library examples the following argument needs to be added:

```
-IDevelop:AmiSSL/Developer/include
```

This will tell the compiler where the additional include files for the SSL library are located.

Instead of providing the locations of the additional include file directories on the command line it is also possible to add them to the vincludesos3: assign. This assign is setup in the S:User-Startup and is used by VBCC to locate the includes it uses. Doing this will save typing, but will slow down compilation of programs that do not actually need access to the networking and/or SSL includes.

Another option, which is more useful for larger projects anyway, is the use of a build system. One example of such a build system is *amake*. It was written for the Amiga from scratch and is available from Aminet:

http://aminet.net/dev/c/amake_v1.00.lha

The program was developed by Alexis Wilke in 1994, which is quite a while ago. It is unlikely to be fully compatible with current versions of *make,* but this is unlikely to be a problem.

Cross-compilation

Using a modern OS to develop Amiga software gives access to more modern editors with syntax colouring and auto-completion, or even full-blown integrated development environments. Cross-compilation also allows for using more modern versions of C++ for example.

The GCC compiler

To test cross-compilation I used amiga-gcc, which is (at the time for writing) still maintained. To test compiling the examples amiga-gcc was installed on a PC running Ubuntu-Mate 24.10. The amiga-gcc system does not only contain the GCC compiler, but also the binutils and various other tools useful for cross-compiling Amiga software.

Amiga-gcc can be found on Stefan 'Bebbo' Franke's GitHub page:

https://github.com/bebbo/amiga-gcc

The installation instructions for the program, the tools and the includes can be found on the same GitHub page. After installation the Amiga GCC compiler is called m68k-amigaos-gcc and can be found in the /opt/amiga/bin/ directory (if the default /opt folder was used).

There is no need to download and install the NDK, it has already been installed as part of the amiga-gcc installation.

AmiSSL

The header files needed for AmiSSL development are not part of the amiga-gcc setup and need to be added separately. To do this first download the latest AmiSSL SDK from its GitHub page:

https://github.com/jens-maus/amissl/releases/

Then unpack the SDK archive and copy all the contents of the *Developer* folder into the *include* folder of the amiga-gcc installation. If the default options were used during installation of amiga-gcc then this should be the /opt/amiga/include folder.

Building the examples with GCC

To build each of the socket library examples the following command is used from the terminal:

```
/opt/amiga/bin/m68k-amigaos-gcc <input> -noixemul -o <output>
```

Where the <output> argument is replaced with the name of the executable and the <input> argument is replaced with the name of the source file. The -noixemul argument ensures that the resulting executable handles its command line arguments as expected by the AmigaOS Shell. Without it the argv[] array will contain pointers to junk.

It is not necessary to provide additional include directory locations since all includes are stored in the same include folder. On a modern system the additional time taken by the compiler to go through all these directories is negligible and barely affects the time of compilation.

2. Networking basics

This chapter looks at the basics of IP networking. How the addressing works, which special addresses exist and how network translation is used to connect the local network with the greater Internet. It concentrates mainly on the things that are of interest to the average Amiga network application programmer.

The physical network

Most people nowadays connect to the Internet via some kind of Broadband. This could be over a cable TV network, ADSL via the phone line or via something like a optical network terminal for a fibre connection. In most cases the modem and the router will be in one device and that device provides wireless network access as well as ports for wired network connections. In other cases there may be two separate devices. For example with fibre optical connections the optical network terminal (ONT) is usually a separate device that is connected to the router via a cable.

The following image shows a simple network setup with an Amiga and a Network Attached Storage (NAS) on the local network.

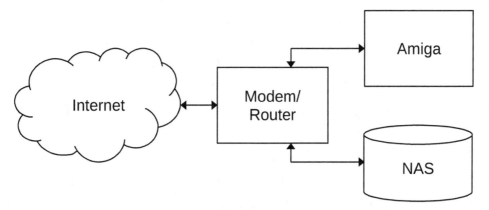

The arrows show the physical connections, which can be wired as well as wireless. The physical connection between the Internet and the modem/router depends on the type of Internet connection used and is out of the scope for this book.

The connections from the router to the rest of the local network tend to be either with cables (Ethernet) or wireless (Wi-Fi). The rest of this section will go into these two types of physical connection a bit more.

Ethernet

The Ethernet standard calls every end point connected to the network a station. This could be a server, a phone, a computer, a thermostat and so on. Anything that is connected to the network in order to communicate is a station.

In the early days of Ethernet multiple stations would share the same coaxial cable as their network connection. This sharing of the cable meant that only one station could send data at one time. If multiple stations tried to send data a collision would occur and the data would get corrupted. Since only one station could be sending on each cable all connections were half-duplex, meaning that two stations that were communicating together always had to wait for each other before starting a return transmission.

Over time the shared coaxial cable was replaced by giving each station on the network its own cable connected to a network switch. This cable is made with a multi-core twisted-pair cable and has an RJ-45 jack on both ends. Since it has separate transmit and receive cable pairs the cable allows for full-duplex communication, where two stations communicating together can both send data to each other at the same time without this causing collisions or data corruption.

MAC address

Each Ethernet station has a pre-programmed 48-bits address called the MAC address. This address is unique to the network interface and can be used by other stations on the network as the address to send data to. There is also a special MAC address that is known as the broadcast address. Any data sent to this address is automatically forwarded to all stations on the network. This can for example be used to discover which station has which MAC address.

The MAC address is only used on the local Ethernet network. It is not used for communication over the Internet. The MAC address of a system that is connected to the Internet can not be used to connect to that system from anywhere else than the local network itself.

The frame

Data is sent as a block of bytes, called a frame. Each frame starts with a header that contains the sender's MAC address, the intended receiver's MAC address and some other protocol dependent data. The header is followed by the payload data, which has a minimum size of 64 bytes and a maximum size of 1500 bytes. If the payload is smaller than 64 bytes then additional padding bytes must be added. After the payload a 4 byte checksum follows. This checksum is known as the frame check sequence or FCS. The FCS is calculated over the header and the payload data so that data corruption can be detected by the receiver.

Switches

All stations are connected to each other via one or more network switches. In a simple home environment the switch is usually built into the Internet router. When a station sends a frame on the network it is received by the switch. The switch will then use the destination MAC address on the frame to send the frame on to the correct station. It has working memory that it uses as a queue so that when multiple stations send frames to the same destination at the same time these can all be forwarded on, one after the other, without collisions. This process is called packet switching, which is where the network switch gets its name from.

This all happens transparently and to all stations it looks like they have a full-duplex connection to each of the other stations on the network.

Wi-Fi

The Wi-Fi standard was created to operate seamlessly with Ethernet and as such can be seen as a sibling standard. Just like with Ethernet every endpoint on the network is called a station. The packets transmitted on the wireless network use the same MAC address based addressing system.

Each station on a Wi-Fi channel will receive all packets that are transmitted on that channel and will ignore the ones it is not interested in. If two stations transmit at the same time on a channel then the signal gets corrupted and the data will be lost. To prevent this from happening only one station can transmit at any one time, which means that Wi-Fi is half-duplex.

Broadband

The router/modem connects to the Internet via a broadband connection. The term broadband is a catch-all term used for connections that are faster than an old fashioned POTS (plain old telephone system) modem and is not the name of a particular technology. The thing that these connections do have in common is that they tend to use a point-to-point protocol to create a link between the router and the network of the Internet service provider. This link could well be using Ethernet together with the PPPoE protocol, which stands for Point-to-Point Protocol over Ethernet. This Ethernet connection is kept completely separate from the Ethernet connections of the local network. The router will not pass the Ethernet frames on like it does on the local network side. Instead it will only pass on the payload of each frame it receives and repackage it into a new frame.

The frame section showed that an Ethernet frame can have a payload of 1500 bytes. Due to additional overhead required by the Point-to-Point protocol the maximal payload size over many PPPoE links is reduced to 1492 bytes.

The IP network

The IP network is built on top of the physical network. The data packets of the IP network are placed into the payload area of the packets that are sent over the physical network. For example, with Ethernet each IP network packet is stored inside the payload area of an Ethernet frame.

The IP network standard does not use the term station like Ethernet does, but instead it calls every end point connected to the IP network a host. And just like with Ethernet's stations, a host can be a computer, server, router, and so on.

The IP address

Each host needs its own unique address so that other hosts can communicate with it. When a computer sends a connection request to a server then not only does the computer needs to know the address of the server to send the request to, the server also needs to know the address of the connecting computer so it knows where to send the answer to.

It is perfectly possible to assign multiple IP addresses to a single network interface, but for the scope of this book it is assumed that a host will only have one IP address per interface.

An IPv4 address consists of 32 bits. For display purposes the IP address is split into 4 bytes of which the values are shown as decimal numbers that are separated by dots. An example of an IP address written out like this is:

```
77.68.10.236
```

The IP address of a host is either setup as a fixed address, known as a static address, or the host is assigned a dynamic address by a server as soon as the host wants to join the network. This is usually done by a dynamic host configuration protocol server, or DHCP server for short. For most people at home the DHCP server is part of their Internet router.

Ports

A host may have a number of different applications running on it that each needs an independent connection. For example a server could be providing a website as well as email on the same system. This is where port numbers come into play. Each application gets its own port number so that anything connecting to the server can then use the port number to connect to the correct application. A lot of standard applications have been given standard port numbers. Web servers use port 80 unless HTTPS encryption is used and then the server is on port 443. Incoming mail following the SMTP standard will be on port 25, while a POP3 mailbox uses port 110. And again the encrypted versions can be on other dedicated port numbers.

The port number can be thought of a bit like a house number. Where the IP address makes sure that the post (i.e. the network traffic) ends up in the right street (host) the port number ensures it ends up at the correct house (application).

Hosts that are not used as servers also need to use ports as there can easily be multiple applications needing network access at the same time. For example a phone could have a web browser running as well as an email program. Each connection will gets its own port number to make sure that the data from the different connections go to the correct application. In most cases this port number will be randomly assigned by the operating system, known as an ephemeral port number.

The port number is a 16 bits unsigned integer and is usually displayed as a single number. In a lot of cases the port number is omitted in the user interface when the default port is used. Web browsers don't show the 80 or 443 in the URL since those are the default values, but internally they will still need to use the correct port number when connecting to the server.

Netmasks

For a system with one single network interface there are roughly two categories of external place a connection could go to. The first category is a host on the same local network. The second category is a host anywhere else, on the Internet at large. The netmask is used to separate these two.

One part of the IP address, known as the network prefix, must be the same for all systems on the local network. The other part of the IP address, known as the host identifier, must be unique for each system on the network. Two IP addresses are on the same local network when their network prefix matches. In IP speak they are on the same subnet. If the network prefix does not match then the address is not on the same network and thus cannot be reached directly but needs to be accessed via a router/gateway.

Which part of the IP address is the network prefix and which part is the host identifier is decided by the netmask. Just like the IP address the netmask is a 32 bits number. For each bit of the netmask that is '1' the corresponding bit of the IP address is part of the network prefix. For each '0' bit of the netmask the corresponding bit of the IP address is the host identifier. The network prefix of an IP address can be calculated by using the netmask to perform a bitwise AND with the IP address.

IP address: `192.168.5.2`

Netmask: `255.255.0.0`

Network prefix: `192.168.0.0`

Host identifier: `0.0.5.2`

There is one special rule for netmasks, which is that the '1' bits start at the left hand side and the '0' bits are on the right. And when (looking from left to right) the switch from '1' to '0' has been made it will stay '0' until the end. In other words, there is only one location in the netmask where there is a '1' bit next to a '0' bit. Some examples:

Valid: 255.255.252.0   255.0.0.0   255.128.0.0   255.255.192.0

Invalid: 252.0.255.255   0.0.0.255   128.255.0.0   255.127.0.0

Traditionally a netmask is also displayed as four decimal numbers that are separated by dots (as shown in the examples above). A more modern way of displaying is by counting the number of '1's in the netmask and placing this number with a '/' at the end of the IP address. For example the address '192.168.0.2' with the netmask of '255.255.0.0' is then written as:

192.168.0.2/16

Which can be read as IP address '192.168.0.2' of which the first 16 bits are the network prefix.

The netmask also defines the range of host addresses available for the local network. For a mask of 255.255.255.0 the first 24 bits are used by the network prefix, which then only leaves the last 8 bits as the host identifier. For a mask of 255.255.0.0 only the first 16 bits are used for the network prefix, leaving 16 bits for the host identifier.

Historically there were different classes of network and the class of network used would decide the netmask. This system of classes was dropped due to the vastly increasing need for IPv4 addresses when the Internet grew in the 1990s. In older documentation it is therefore not unusual to read about class 'A', 'B' or 'C' networks, but that is no longer relevant to how the Internet works.

The broadcast address

For certain protocols it is necessary to have an address that can be used to communicate with all hosts on the local network. This address is called the broadcast address. An example of this the Address Resolution Protocol or ARP, which is used to find a particular host on the local network. It does this by broadcasting a request for the host with a particular IP address to identify itself, "which one of you is 192.168.0.23?". Hosts with a different IP address can ignore the request and the host with the requested IP address can respond.

The broadcast address used by IPv4 networks is the last address in the range, the one where all bits of the host identifier part are set to '1'. Here are some examples:

IP address	netmask	Broadcast address
192.168.10.2	255.255.0.0	192.168.255.255
192.168.10.2	255.255.255.0	192.168.10.255

There is another broadcast address, one that does not depend on the actual address range. It is the address with all bits set to '1': 255.255.255.255. This address is used when the host does not have an IP address yet. One use for example is DHCP where the host is using this broadcast address to request a dynamic IP address from the DHCP server on the local network.

Broadcasting is only meant for the local network and as a result routers do not pass broadcast traffic on to the Internet, they will only pass it on to the local hosts.

Reserved host addresses

The host address with all bits set to '1' (the broadcast address) and the host address with all bits set to '0' cannot be assigned to a host as a normal IP address. Therefore in each subnet there will be two of these reserved addresses that cannot be assigned to a host. In a subnet with netmask 255.255.255.0 there are 256 addresses, but there can be no more than 254 hosts.

Special address ranges

A number of address ranges have been reserved for special use cases. The most widely used set of these address ranges are the ranges set aside for local networks. These addresses are safe to be used on a local network since no host on the Internet will be using these. There are three of these ranges available. The one with the smallest number of hosts seems to be the most popular with router manufacturers for their default setup.

Address	Netmask	Range	Hosts
192.168.0.0	255.255.0.0	192.168.0.0 - 192.168.255.255	65534
172.16.0.0	255.192.0.0	172.16.0.0 - 172.31.255.255	1048574
10.0.0.0	255.0.0.0	10.0.0.0 - 10.255.255.255	16777214

Sometimes an application needs to be able to connect to another application on the same host. For this reason the 127.0.0.0/255.0.0.0 range has been reserved. Applications can use 127.0.0.1 to connect to other applications on the same host without having to look up what the actual IP address is of the host. The address is assigned to the loopback interface, which is a virtual interface that is treated like a completely separate interface from the actual network interface.

Another range of addresses is set aside for multicasting. This is where one host can send data that will be received by multiple hosts without having to make individual connections between the sending host and each of the receiving hosts. This works a bit like broadcasting but in this case each receiving host needs to sign up to receive the data. This allows intelligent switches and routers on the network to limit the traffic to only go to the hosts that requested it. The multicast address range is from 224.0.0.0 until 239.255.255.255.

Network Address Translation

The local address ranges are used all over the world. However, when a host with local address 192.168.0.2 connects to a server on the Internet the server needs to know where to send the response to. And there could be thousands and thousands of hosts that have this particular address on their local network. This is where Network Address Translation (or NAT for short) comes in.

When an Internet router connects to the Internet it will be assigned an IP address by the Internet Service Provider (ISP). This IP address will be unique, the router will be the only device in the world with this IP address. This unique IP address is also known as the public IP address since any host on the Internet can use it to connect to. The local address is known as a private address since only hosts on the same local network can connect to it.

Please note that there are exceptions where the address the router gets from the ISP is not actually a public IP address, e.g. when the ISP itself uses NAT to connect their own network to the actual Internet. These situations are out of the scope of this section.

The host on the local network checks the IP address of the server it wants to connect to and determines that it is not on the local network. It will then send the connection request to the Internet router that it knows as its gateway. The router will pass the connection request on to the server on the Internet. However, instead of using the private IP address of the host the router will use the public IP address it got assigned. The server receives the request and sends the response back to the IP address it came from, which is the public IP address of the router. When the response arrives the router will replace the public IP address in the response with the local IP address of the host and then pass the answer on to the host. This replacing of the IP address is the translating bit of NAT.

For outgoing connections (the situation described above) the router knows where to send the responses since it previously handled the outgoing connection request. It keeps a list of the outgoing connections so that it can pass on any responses to the correct hosts on the local network. Incoming connections originate from outside the local network and start with the router receiving a connection request on its public IP address. The router will not know for which local host the request is intended, unless the user has setup a port forwarding rule on the router. If the connection request is for a port that has a forwarding rule then the router will pass on the request to the host the rule tells it to use. If there is no such rule then the router will not be able to pass the request on and will drop it. Depending on the router's configuration it may return an error to the sending host or it may just quietly ignore the request without any notification to the sender. Some router manufacturers give different names to this functionality and use terms like like services or servers on the router's setup pages.

Domain names

While it is very simple for a computer to remember a 32 bits IP address, for us humans it comes less natural. Our strength lies more in remembering words and phrases. It is easier to remember 'google.com', 'aminet.net' and 'amiga.addict.media' than their respective IP addresses. When a user types a domain name then the host software will need to convert this domain name into an IP address before it can be used to communicate with the remote host. This process of conversion is called resolving and is done by sending a name server a request to resolve the domain name.

A domain name can have multiple addresses associated with it since the mail server for the domain name could be on a different IP address than the web server. These different addresses are stored on the domain server as different records. To get the IPv4 web address of a server the 'A' record is required, while getting the same domain name's mail server requires the 'MX' record.

Making connections

Before a host can connect to a host on the Internet a number of things need to have happened first. This section goes through the things happening on the physical network as well as the IP network to get the host to connect to a server.

The image below shows a simple hypothetical local network setup that will be used in this section.

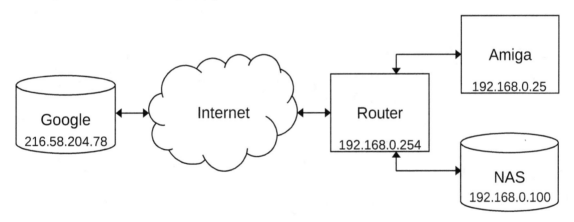

Powering up

When the router is powered up it will setup its local network with the fixed IP address that it was configured with. It then will prepare its DHCP server with the pool of addresses to be used. At the same time it will also establish the physical connection with the Internet and acquire a public IP address from the ISP that it will use on the Internet connection.

The Amiga is also powered up and it needs to contact the DHCP server to get a dynamic IP address. To do this it broadcasts a DHCP request on the 255.255.255.255 broadcast address. The router's DHCP server receives the request and replies to the Amiga with the 192.168.0.25 address, which the Amiga will now use. The reply will also contain the address of a name server to use for resolving domain names and the IP address of the gateway. These usually both are the address of the router itself. Since the reply is received via Ethernet the Amiga now also knows the MAC address of the router and the router now also knows the MAC address of the Amiga.

Connecting to the NAS

The file transfer application on the Amiga has the IP address of the NAS already configured. It passes the connection request for address 192.168.0.100 on to the network stack. The network stack will compare this address with its own address and netmask and concludes that the NAS is on the same local network. Then it will send out an ARP request for 192.168.0.100 using the Ethernet broadcast address.

The NAS receives the request and sends its response back to the Ethernet MAC address of the station that sent the request (the Amiga). The NAS now knows the MAC address of the Amiga as well as its IP address. When the Amiga receives the response of the NAS it gets the MAC address that goes with the IP address of the NAS.

Since both sides of the connection now know each other's MAC address they can from now on send each other Ethernet frames directly. The networking switch that is part of the router will pass on the Ethernet frames between the two without interfering.

The Amiga can now send the IP protocol connection request to the NAS. The NAS can respond to it and both can transfer data between each other over the local network. This will all be over Ethernet, with the IP packets inside the payload area of the Ethernet frames and the frames will be routed according to the MAC addresses.

Connecting to Google

The user of the Amiga types 'google.com' in the address bar of a browser. The Amiga now needs to resolve the domain name into an IP address and then connect to it. From the DHCP server it received the IP address of the name server to use, which is the IP address of the router itself.

The Amiga's network stack will compare the IP address of the name server (which is the same as the router's IP address) with its own address and netmask and conclude that it is on the same local network. The Amiga also already has the MAC address that goes with the IP address. It can therefore immediately send the request to resolve the domain name to the name server.

The name server on the router then resolves the domain name into an IP address. It may need to connect to the name servers of the ISP to do this or to name servers on the Internet. When it has the IP address it can send the answer back to the Amiga using the Amiga's MAC address.

The Amiga now knows the IP address of one of the Google web servers, 216.58.204.78. When comparing it with its own IP address and netmask it is clear that this is not on the local network. The Amiga therefore needs to use the router as its gateway to the Internet. The Amiga will send the connection request to IP address 216.58.204.78 but use the MAC address of the router on the Ethernet frames. The router will receive the request and repackage it for sending it to the Internet. It will also replace the Amiga's address of 192.168.0.25 in the IP header with its own public IP address so that the Google server knows where to send the reply.

The Google server receives the connection request and returns its reply to the IP address of the sender. The reply will therefore end up back at the router. The router receives the reply and since it has sent out the original request it knows which local host the reply is for. It repackages the reply into an Ethernet frame, which it gives the MAC address of the Amiga as the destination address. The router also changes the destination address in the IP header from the public IP address into the Amiga's local IP address (192.168.0.25). It then sends the frame onto the local network.

The Amiga network stack receives the frame since it has its MAC address as the destination. It checks the IP address in the IP header and sees it is correct as well. It then passes the reply from the web server on to the web browser.

Assuming that the connection was successfully established all further traffic for this connection between the Amiga and the Google server will now follow this established path.

3. IP Networking

This chapter will look closely at the way the IP protocols work. In the case of the Amiga only the older IP version 4 is currently supported by the various network stacks. Therefore this chapter will only look at the protocols that are part of IPv4. This is not a huge issue since IPv4 is in 2025 still the most widely used version, even though IPv6 is getting more traction.

Most of the details shown in this chapter are taken care of by the network stack and are therefore not directly required knowledge when programming networking applications. However, knowing what happens 'under the hood' so to speak is still very useful. Please note that many small details have been left out for brevity reasons.

When sending data on the network it is important to know in which order the bits need to be sent. This is known as the network order, which may not be the same as the ordering used by the host, known as the host order. In the case of the 680x0 family of processors the network order is exactly the same as the host order, with the most significant bit stored at the left and the least significant bit stored at the right hand side of each field. On Intel based systems this is not the case and as a result Intel network code uses the ntoh() / hton() functions to convert between the orders.

The IP header

All protocols used by IPv4 share the same header structure and simply expand on it by adding fields as required. The IP header is added to the start of every single packet that the IP network stack transmits. The base header shared by all IPv4 protocols looks as follows:

0										1										2										3	
0	1	2	3	4	5	6	7	8	9	0	1	2	3	4	5	6	7	8	9	0	1	2	3	4	5	6	7	8	9	0	1
Version				IHL				Type of service								Total length															
Identification																Flags			Fragment offset												
Time to live								Protocol								Header checksum															
Source address																															
Destination address																															
[Options]																															

The header of the protocol itself will directly follow this header.

Version - The version number in four bits, for IPv4 this field will contain the number 4.

IHL - Internet Header Length, the length of this header expressed in the number of 32 bits words. The minimum value for this field is 5 (20 bytes), which is correct when there are no options added to this header.

Type of service - This 8 bit field was initially used to indicate the type of service required. The routers that pass the packet would use the field to decide which route it should take. The field has be re-purposed a couple of times and is now cleared/ignored by some Internet service providers.

Total length - The length of the packet in bytes, including the header as well as the data. The maximum value that can be fitted into this 16 bits field is 65535. However, there is no guarantee that the network stack will be able to handle a packet of this size. The IPv4 standard states that all hosts must be able to handle packets of 576 bytes in size.

Identification - When a too large packet needs to be fragmented then this field is used to mark the fragments. Each fragment that is part of the same packet will receive the same identification number so that the receiving router/host knows which fragments belong to which packet.

Flags - Three control flags:
> Bit 0 - Must be set to zero.
> Bit 1 - DF (Don't Fragment). When set to 1 the packet is not allowed to be fragmented.
> Bit 2 - MF (More Fragments). Set to 1 if there are more fragments.

Fragment offset - Used by fragments to indicate where in the original packet the data of this fragment was located. The very first fragment will have an offset of zero. This 13 bits field counts in numbers of 8 byte blocks.

Time to live - Also known as the TTL. Originally the number of seconds a packet is allowed to exist but normally implemented as a counter that is decreased by each router that passes the packet on. When the TTL reaches zero the packet is not passed on to the next router but instead it is dropped. This limits the range of the packet and can be used to ensure that packets stay within the boundary of a local network.

Protocol - This 8 bit number identifies the IP protocol used. Examples are UDP and TCP.

Header checksum - A 16 bits checksum calculated over the fields of the header. When the checksum is calculated a value of 0 is used for the checksum field. Each time a field of the header is changed (the TTL for example) a new checksum must be calculated

Source address - The 32 bits IP address of the host sending the packet.

Destination address - The 32 bits IP address of the host the packet is intended for.

Options - This field is optional but if it is present must always be padded to a byte length divisible by 4. If the IHL value is larger than 5 then this means that the options field is present. The options field is not often used and some of the options are now considered a security risk and some routers will drop any packets containing those options.

Fragmentation

When a packet is too large to be passed on to the next router it can be split up into smaller packets called fragments. If the DF (don't fragment) flag is set in the flags field of a packet's header then fragmenting is not allowed and the packet will need to be dropped.

When a packet is fragmented the first fragment will have the MF (more fragments) flag set and will have its fragment offset field set to zero. The last fragment will have the MF flag cleared and will have the fragment offset field set to the location where the data in the fragment should go when recreating the original packet. Any fragments that go between the first and the last will have the MF flag set and have a value in their fragment offset field. This is shown in the following image, where a packet with 768 bytes of data is fragmented into 3 fragments with 256 bytes of data each:

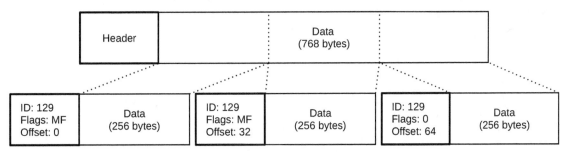

All fragments that are part of the same packet will have the same 16 bits identification value. Each fragment may follow a different route due to congestion, load balancing or other routing demands. The result of this is that the fragments may not be received in the same order as they were sent out and fragments of other packets may be mixed in. The identification field allows the re-assembler to pick the correct fragments from all the fragments received to reassemble the original packet.

The receiver of the fragmented packets may also be receiving fragments belonging to multiple connections from multiple senders. This can lead to overlap in the identification values. When a packet is reassembled not only the identification field is used, the protocol, source address and destination address fields are also used to ensure that all fragments are part of the same packet.

Fragmenting makes the data transfer less efficient since it worsens the ratio between header data and actual data. It can also increase the impact of packet loss on reliable protocols like TCP, where the loss of one single fragment will cause the retransmission of the whole original packet.

User Datagram Protocol

The User Datagram Protocol (UDP) is the simplest of the IP protocols. It is based around packets of data called datagrams. There is no connection mechanism; the datagram has the address and port of the intended recipient host in its header and is transmitted on the network. This is similar to putting an address on an postcard and posting it in the mail.

There is no guarantee that the datagram will arrive at its destination and the protocol provides no feedback to the sender. Routers may for example drop the datagram if they are running out of bandwidth. If it is important for the sender to have some kind of feedback then this needs to be implemented by the sender/receiver application on top of UDP. This is similar to the recipient of a postcard calling the sender to say that their card has arrived.

When the datagram is received it will be exactly the same as it was sent. No data will have been added and no data will have been removed. Either the whole datagram is received or nothing. It is also possible that the same datagram will be received more than once. When multiple datagrams are sent to the same destination then it is possible that they arrive in a different order than they were sent out. One or more could be missing, one or more could be received more than once. This is shown in the below image where datagram 12 and 13 have swapped positions, datagram 15 was received twice and datagram 14 has not (yet?) arrived:

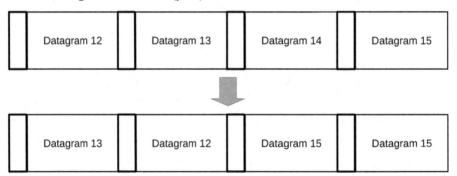

Applications using UDP for communication need to take all these issues into account. In a lot of cases this is quite straightforward. The DNS system uses UDP where the request to resolve a domain name is sent as a UDP datagram to one or more name servers. The name servers then respond to the request by sending the answer in a UDP datagram addressed to the requesting host. If the requesting host does not receive an answer within a short time period then it will send out the datagram again. This covers the case where either the requesting datagram or the answer datagram got lost. If there is still no answer after a couple of tries then the DNS server may be inactive or the connection between the host and the name server is down.

The header

The header used by UDP is added directly behind the general IP header shown at the start of this chapter. The actual data will be following immediately after the UDP header. The value for the protocol field in the IP header is 11 to indicate that the User Datagram Protocol is being used.

0										1										2										3	
0	1	2	3	4	5	6	7	8	9	0	1	2	3	4	5	6	7	8	9	0	1	2	3	4	5	6	7	8	9	0	1
Source port																Destination port															
Length																Checksum															
Data...																															

Source port - The sender's 16 bits port number that can be used to send a reply to. If no reply is expected or needed then this field can be set to zero.

Destination port - The port number on the receiving host the datagram is intended for.

Length - The length of the datagram in bytes. This includes the amount of data as well as the length of the 8 byte UDP header. It does not include the length of the IP header.

Checksum - A 16 bit checksum calculated over a pseudo header as well as the data of the datagram (see section below). Can be set to zero to indicate that no checksum was calculated.

Checksum calculation

The checksum is calculated over the UDP header and the data as well as the following pseudo IP header. This pseudo IP header is used as if it was prefixed to the UDP header.

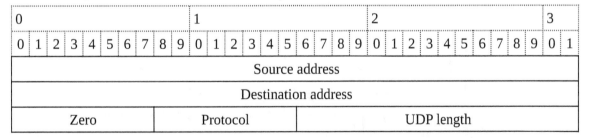

0										1										2										3	
0	1	2	3	4	5	6	7	8	9	0	1	2	3	4	5	6	7	8	9	0	1	2	3	4	5	6	7	8	9	0	1
Source address																															
Destination address																															
Zero										Protocol										UDP length										

The reason for doing it this way is that the fields in the real IP header will be changing (like the time to live value) and this would mean that the UDP checksum needs to be recalculated each time as well. By including only important unchanging fields the routers along the way can ignore the UDP checksum and leave that to the receiving host.

The checksum is calculated by creating a 1's complement sum of all the 16 bit words of the pseudo header, the UDP header and the data. If the data is not an even number of bytes a zero byte needs to be added as padding. If the result of the calculation happens to be zero then a value of all ones needs to be used instead since a value of zero is reserved for signalling that no checksum is used.

Transmission Control Protocol

The Transmission Control Protocol (TCP) is in many ways the opposite of the UDP protocol. It is based around a connection and there is communication between the sender and the receiver to control the flow of data. This flow of data is known as the stream. If the data is larger than what fits inside one network packet the protocol will use as many packets as necessary to transmit the data. A packet is referred to as a segment within the parlance of TCP since each packet is just a segment of the overall stream of data. The protocol ensures that on the receiving end all data is received in the correct order and that there will be no duplication. The protocol also takes care of error checking as well as retransmission of missing or damaged segments.

On their way over the network the segments may be reorganised by routers. It is therefore possible that an application sends the data in 4 segments, each containing 128 bytes of data, while the receiver only sees one segment containing 512 bytes of data. These 512 bytes will be in the same order as the 4 times 128 bytes were sent and none of the data will be missing or duplicated. However, it is important to note this when receiving TCP data; an application can make no assumptions on how the data will be packaged when it is received.

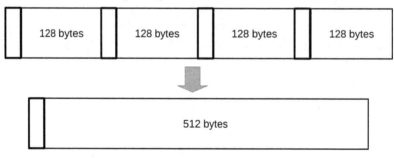

When a segment is damaged or missing then TCP will hold off sending the next segment. For how long it will hold off depends on how often segments go missing and how many segments have already been missing on the connection. Holding off sending out segments increases delivery time (latency), which makes TCP less useful for real-time communication where a short delivery time is key. Two-way communication protocols like VOIP therefore usually rely on UDP instead of TCP. Delivery time is less important for one-way delivery, which is for example why radio streaming on the Internet is based on TCP and uses a large receiving buffer on the client side.

To create a connection one host will be listening for incoming connection requests. The other host will send out the connection request to the listening host. An example of this is a web server listening for connections on one host and the web browser connecting to it on another host. After the connection has been established the two hosts have a bidirectional pipe where both can send and receive data. The web browser will use this pipe to send a 'get request' for a particular URL, the server will then use this same pipe to send the requested data. The host that sent out the connection request (the browser) is said to have an active connection, while the host that accepted the incoming connection request (the web server) is said to have a passive connection.

The header

The header used by TCP is added directly behind the general IP header shown at the start of this chapter. The actual data will be following immediately after the TCP header. The value for the protocol field in the IP header is 7 to indicate that the Transmission Control Protocol is being used.

0										1										2										3	
0	1	2	3	4	5	6	7	8	9	0	1	2	3	4	5	6	7	8	9	0	1	2	3	4	5	6	7	8	9	0	1
Source port																Destination port															
Sequence number																															
Acknowledgement number																															
Data offset				Reserved				CWR	ECE	URG	ACK	PSH	RST	SYN	FIN	Window															
Checksum																Urgent pointer															
[Options]																															
Data…																															

Source port - The sender's 16 bits port number. This field can not be set to zero.

Destination port - The port number used by the remote host.

Sequence number - The sequence number of the first data byte in this segment.

Acknowledgement number - The value of the next sequence number that the host sending this segment expects to receive. This field is only valid if the ACK flag has been set.

Data offset - A 4 bit value denoting the number of 32 bit words used by the TCP header. This can be used to find out where the data starts and if there are any options in the header.

Reserved - These four bits should be set to zero. They are used by modern extensions.

Flags - A number of control bits:

       0 - CWR - Congestion Window Reduced.

       1 - ECE - ECN Echo.

       2 - URG - Urgent pointer field is significant.

       3 - ACK - Acknowledgement number field is significant.

       4 - PSH - Push function.

       5 - RST - Reset the connection.

       6 - SYN - Synchronise sequence numbers.

       7 - FIN - No more data from this sender.

Window - The number of bytes this host is willing to receive. This is an unsigned 16 bits number. The sequence number of the first byte of this window is set in the Acknowledgement Number field.

Checksum - A 16 bit checksum calculated over a pseudo header as well as the data of the segment (see section below). Unlike with UDP, this field must always be calculated.

Urgent pointer - This value is a 16 bits positive offset calculated from the sequence number in this segment and points to the first byte of urgent data. This field is only valid if the URG flag has been set. Using urgent data is discouraged by the current version of the TCP standard.

Options - Options may or may not be present. If present then the Data offset value will be larger than 5. Since a TCP header has to be a multiple of 32 bit words the options may need to be padded.

Checksum calculation

The checksum is calculated over the TCP header and the data as well as the pseudo IP header shown below. This pseudo header is used as if it was prefixed to the TCP header. The reason for doing it this way is that other fields in the real IP header will be changing (like the time to live value) and this would mean that the TCP checksum needs to be recalculated each time as well. By including only important unchanging fields the routers along the way can ignore the TCP checksum and leave checking that to the receiving host.

0										1										2										3	
0	1	2	3	4	5	6	7	8	9	0	1	2	3	4	5	6	7	8	9	0	1	2	3	4	5	6	7	8	9	0	1
Source address																															
Destination address																															
Zero										Protocol										TCP length											

The checksum is calculated by creating a 1's complement sum of all the 16 bit words of the pseudo header, the TCP header and the data. If the data is not an even number of bytes then a zero byte needs to be added as padding.

Sequence numbers

The sequence numbers are used to ensure that data is in the correct order, that there is no missing data and that no data is duplicated. The sequence number is incremented with each byte sent where the first byte of data in a segment has the sequence number shown in the sequence number field of the header of the segment. For example, if the current segment has number 250 and there are 50 bytes of data in the segment then the next segment will have number 300. Since TCP connections are bidirectional there is an independent sequence number for each direction.

For security purposes the segment number does not start at a fixed value. The starting number is derived from using a secret key as well as the local IP address and port and the remote IP address and port as seeds for a pseudorandom function. The result from this function is then added to a value from a clock that increments approximately once every 4 milliseconds. This algorithm ensures that different connections get very different starting sequence numbers and even when the same connection is being made again the clock value will have moved on, ensuring that the next connection does not again use the same starting sequence number.

Since the segment number is a 32 bits unsigned integer it may roll over during the connection, depending on how much data was sent and at which value the numbering started. The number rolling over is not a problem since there either were never any segments on this connection with numbers that low, or if there were then this is long enough ago not to expect any of them to be still on their way on the network.

Connecting

To create a connection the active host will send a single fragment to the host it wants to connect to. This segment will have the initial segment number in the segment number field and has the SYN flag set. There will be no actual data in the segment.

The host that receives this segment, the passive host, will reply by sending a single segment back to the active host. This segment will have the initial segment number of the passive host in the segment number field (which will be a different number than the one used by the active host) and will have the SYN flag set. To acknowledge the active host's segment number the ACK flag will also be set and the acknowledgement number field will contain the active host's acknowledgement number incremented by one. Again, no actual data will be present in the segment.

When the active host receives this segment it will respond by sending a segment that has the sequence number field set to one more than the previous segment it sent (since the SYN segment is seen as occupying a space of 1). The ACK flag is set and the acknowledgement number field is set to the passive segment number plus one.

From that moment on the 3 way handshake is complete and both sides can start sending data. The sequence numbers used for this data are the same as the ones used for the ACK segments, since the ACKs do not require sequence numbers to go up.

The following image shows the handshake in action:

	Active host status	Header field values	Passive host status
1	CLOSED		LISTEN
2	SYN-SENT ➡	<SEQ=400><Flag=SYN>	➡ SYN-RECEIVED
3	ESTABLISHED ⬅	<SEQ=150><ACK=401><Flag=SYN,ACK> ⬅	SYN-RECEIVED
4	ESTABLISHED ➡	<SEQ=401><ACK=151><Flag=ACK>	➡ ESTABLISHED
5	ESTABLISHED ➡	<SEQ=401><ACK=151><Flag=ACK><DATA>	➡ ESTABLISHED

Disconnecting

There are two methods of closing a connection. The first method is by sending a segment with the RST flag set. This resets the connection, which means that both sides of the connection go back to the state they were in prior to creating the connection. Any data that has not been acknowledged may be lost.

The second method is a more controlled way of disconnecting that does not lead to data loss. At some point during the connection one of the hosts (host A) will have sent all data and no longer needs to send any more. It signals this to the other host (B) by setting the FIN flag in the last segment it sends. The FIN segment uses one single number in the segment number space, which allows host B to acknowledge it. At this point all data sent by host A has been successfully received and acknowledged by host B.

From here on no more data will be sent from host A to host B, but host B can continue to send data to host A and host A can continue to send segments (without data) to ACK the received data. When host B has sent all its data it will also send a segment with the FIN flag set, which also uses a single segment number. Host A responds with a single segment that ACKs the reception of the FIN segment to host B. Now that both hosts have sent FIN segments and received ACKs for these segments they can both close the connection. All data has been acknowledged and therefore both hosts know that no data was lost.

Data transfer

The sequence number in each segment header relates to the first byte of data that is in the segment. The sender will increment the sequence number for every byte transferred. For example, if the sequence number is 150 and the segment contains 250 bytes of data then the next segment will have the number 400 in the sequence number field. The receiver will keep track of the number of bytes received so far and places the sequence number of the next byte it expects to receive in the Acknowledgement number field. The receiver will also use the sequence number of the incoming segments to filter out duplicated segments and uses the checksum to discard damaged segments.

When the sender receives the acknowledgement number from the receiver it knows how much data has been received successfully and that it can remove this data from its internal buffers as no retransmissions will be needed. The sender also uses the received acknowledgement number to determine if previously sent data needs to be retransmitted. If this is the case then the sender will hold off transmitting for a period. This period will increase each time there is another retransmission. The sender will also retransmit segments when no acknowledgement is received from the receiver to prevent communication stalling when either the data segment or the segment carrying the acknowledgement is lost.

The receiver will use the Window field to indicate how much data it is able to accept. If the sender sends more data than the receiver can accept it is likely to be discarded and that will make it necessary to be retransmitted. When data starts to fill up the internal buffers of the receiver the window values it returns to the sender will become smaller. This will allow the sender to match its sending speed with the ability of the receiver to accept the data.

Segmenting

Each segment requires at least 40 bytes of header space comprising of a minimum 20 bytes for the IP header as well as another minimum of 20 bytes for the TCP header. This makes sending small amounts of data very inefficient as most of the data bandwidth will be used up by header bytes instead of data bytes. To make sending small amounts of data more efficient the Nagle algorithm is used, (which is named after its inventor; John Nagle). The algorithm will hold off sending out small amounts of data until enough data has been collected to send out a segment. To ensure that this does not take too long the algorithm will also immediately send out all collected data when the receiver has acknowledged all previously sent data.

A segment also cannot be too large since this will cause it to be fragmented, which also adversely affects the efficiency. The previous chapter showed that the underlying physical network may have a maximum packet size. The network stack will therefore need to ensure that the segments it transmits will fit in the maximum transmission unit (MTU) for the current connection. Different connections may be routed along different networks and links and therefore can have differing maximum packet sizes.

Internet Control Message Protocol

The Internet Control Message Protocol (ICMP) is used by hosts (including routers) to provide feedback, usually in the form of error messages when packets cannot be delivered. ICMP is build on top of IP like the other protocols are, but it is not actually a separate protocol. ICMP is a part of the IP standard and must be implemented in every IP network stack. The main purpose of the ICMP messages is to provide information about problems along the network. There is no guarantee that every lost packet will result in an ICMP message, nor is there any mechanism to prevent ICMP messages from getting lost themselves.

To limit the number of ICMP messages generated the ICMP messages themselves will not generate other ICMP messages (unless the ICMP message is an echo request). If the ICMP message is caused by a fragmented packet then only the first fragment (with the fragment offset field set to 0) will generate a message while none of the other fragments will.

The message

The ICMP message is added directly behind the general IP header. The value for the protocol field in the IP header is 1 to indicate that the Internet Control Message Protocol is being used. The source address in the IP header will be the address of the host that created the message.

0										1										2										3	
0	1	2	3	4	5	6	7	8	9	0	1	2	3	4	5	6	7	8	9	0	1	2	3	4	5	6	7	8	9	0	1
Type								Code								Checksum															
Type dependent																															

Type - The type of ICMP message. Some of the rest of the data in the message depends on the value of the type field.

Code - Depends on the type. For example to add more detail to an error code.

Checksum - A 16 bits checksum calculated over the fields of the header and the data. When calculating the checksum a value of 0 is used for the checksum field. If the type dependent data is an odd number of bytes a zero padding byte should be added for calculation.

Messages types

The following sections will highlight a small number of ICMP messages that are frequently used on the Internet. Please note that this is by no means an exhaustive list of all message types supported by ICMP.

Destination unreachable

This message is sent by the host or gateway that is not able to deliver a datagram or segment to its intended destination.

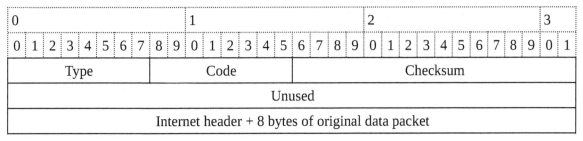

Type - The Destination Unreachable message uses a value of 3.

Code - Reason for the destination being unreachable. Some reasons include:

> 0 - The network is unreachable. The destination is not local and cannot be reached.

> 1 - Host unreachable. The destination host does not exist or is not active.

> 2 - Protocol unreachable. The destination exists but does not support the selected protocol.

> 3 - Port unreachable. The destination host exists but is not accepting data on this port.

> 4 - Fragmentation needed and DF is set. Packet is dropped as no fragmentation is allowed.

Following the 8 bytes of the ICMP header is the Internet header as well as 8 bytes of the original packet that caused the destination unreachable message. This data is included to allow the receiver of the message to find the process the message is intended for.

Time exceeded

This message is usually sent by a gateway when the time to live value of a packet reaches 0 and the packet is therefore discarded. It can also be sent by a host or gateway when a packet is fragmented and reassembling can't be done within its time limit, possibly because not all fragments have been received in time.

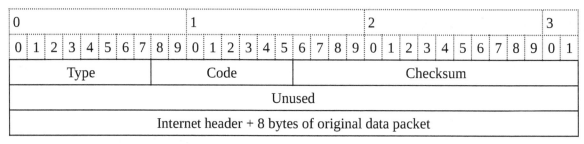

Type - The Time Exceeded message has a type of 11.

Code - The reason for the message:

    0 - The time to live value reached zero.

    1 - The reassembly of fragments exceeded its time limit.

Following the 8 bytes of the ICMP header is the Internet header as well as 8 bytes of the original packet that caused the time exceeded message. This data is included to allow the receiver of the message to find the process the message is intended for.

Echo request and reply

These messages are used to check if a host or gateway is available. Examples of the use of these messages are the ping and traceroute commands. Please note that for security reasons a number of Internet facing systems have disabled replying to echo request messages.

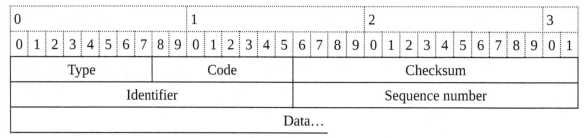

Type - 8 for the Echo Request message, 0 for the Echo Reply message.

Code - Set to 0.

Identifier - Used by the sender to identify this sequence of Echo Request messages.

Sequence number - Used by the sender to identify this particular message in a sequence.

When the destination system receives the message it generates the reply by swapping the source and destination addresses and changing the Type value from 8 to 0. It is then sent back including all the data that was part of the message. Before sending it back the checksum will need to be recalculated as well.

Internet Group Management Protocol

The Internet Group Management Protocol (IGMP) is used by hosts and routers to manage multicast traffic. Multicast allows one host to send the same data to multiple hosts without having to send to each receiver individually. Hosts that want to receive the multicast indicate this by joining the multicast group. The routers will then pass the same traffic on to each host that is part of this multicast group. Regardless of the number of receivers, the sending host only has to send out the data once, the routers on the network then ensure that the data is passed on to all the hosts that joined the multicast group. When a host no longer needs to receive the multicast it can leave the multicast group and the routers will then stop passing on the multicast traffic to that particular host.

The difference with broadcasting is that with multicast the data only goes to the hosts that have joined the group, where as broadcast traffic is sent to all hosts on the network.

Only UDP traffic is suitable for multicasting since it is uni-directional by nature and does not require the receiving hosts to message back at the sending host. The router can copy the datagrams from the sending host into the network links of all receiving hosts verbatim.

With TCP traffic simply copying the same segments to all the receiving hosts is not possible. For example, each receiver may be using different window sizes and miss different packets, therefore expecting different sequence numbers. To deal with this would require a separate connection between the sending host and each receiver, which defeats the object of multicasting.

Unfortunately IPv4 multicast traffic is not supported by the Internet. Most Internet routers will filter out multicast data and not pass it on to the Internet. And even if it was passed on the ISP is then most likely to filter it out too. This means that multicast can only be used on the local network and other local networks that are connected to it via a local router or a VPN that supports multicast.

The message

The IGMP message is added directly behind the general IP header. The value for the protocol field in the IP header is 2 to indicate that the Internet Group Management Protocol is being used. The source address will be the address of the host or gateway that created the message. The time-to-live field of the IP header should be set to 1 for IGMP messages.

0		1		2		3
0 1 2 3 4 5 6 7	8 9 0 1 2 3 4 5	6 7 8 9 0 1 2 3 4 5 6 7 8 9 0 1
Type	Max response time	Checksum
Group address		

Type - The type of message.

> 0x11 - Membership query.
>
> 0x12 - Version 1 membership report (obsolete).
>
> 0x16 - Version 2 membership report.
>
> 0x17 - Leave group.

Max response time - The maximum time before sending an answer in units of 1/10th of a second. Only used by message type 0x11, should be zero for the other types.

Checksum - A 16 bits checksum calculated over the IGMP message. When calculating the checksum a value of 0 is used for the checksum field.

Group address - The address of the multicast group the message is for. Multicast addresses are in the range 224.0.0.0 to 239.255.255.255. If the message type does not require an address then this field is set to zero.

Membership query

Membership query messages are sent out by routers to find out which multicast groups are in use by the hosts on the network. The hosts that are part of a group respond by sending a report. There are two types of membership query. The general query has the group address field set to all zeros and is sent to address 224.0.0.1, which is known as the all hosts address. The group-specific message has the group address field set to the address of the multicast group and is then sent to the multicast group.

The response time field is set to the amount of time (in units of 1/10th of a second) the sender expects between answers. Larger values will reduce the amount of traffic on the network, while lower values will ensure faster responses when hosts leave a group.

Membership report

When a host wants to join a multicast group it will immediately send out a membership report. The membership report message will have the group address field set to the address of the multicast group to join and the report is sent to this same multicast group.

The host will also send out a membership report in response to a membership query from a router. When a host stops sending out membership reports in response to membership queries the router will assume that the host is no longer part of the multicast group.

Leave group

This message is sent by a host when it no longer wants to be part of a multicast group. The leave group message will have the group address field set to the address of the multicast group to leave and the message is sent to 224.0.0.2, which is known as the all routers address.

Version 1 of the IGMP standard did not have a leave group message and instead relied on the membership reports to determine if a host was still needing the multicast or not. If the membership query used a high response time this could lead to a lot of unnecessary bandwidth use. Version 2 of the IGMP standard therefore added the leave group message so that hosts can now immediately stop the multicast from being sent to them.

4. The Socket API

The TCP/IP stack's network programming interface uses an abstraction called a socket to provide access to its functionality. Sockets are quite similar to file handles - on Unix based operating systems sockets are file descriptors and can be used with ordinary file functions. Sockets were introduced by ARPANET, which later became the Internet. Most modern operating systems use a socket API that is based on the implementation of version 4.2 of a Unix variant called the Berkley Software Distribution, or BSD for short.

The Amiga network stacks also use the BSD style socket API, which can be accessed via the aptly named "bsdsocket.library". This library contains functions that are found in most socket implementations as well as functions that are Amiga specific. The Amiga specific functions follow the Amiga naming convention and have a name written in CamelCase, while the other functions follow the BSD convention and are all written in lowercase. Even though there exist a number of different network stacks for the Amiga, this book will use the singular 'stack' for simplicity.

Just like on other operating systems, on the Amiga a socket is used via a handle, known as the socket descriptor. But in the case of the Amiga this descriptor is not a standard file handle and therefore can't be used with the file functions provided by the dos.library.

Each time a process opens the bsdsocket.library a new library base is constructed in memory. This library base can only be used by the process that opened the library. Sharing the library pointer within multiple processes is therefore not supported. Each process that needs access to the bsdsocket.library must obtain its own pointer by calling Exec's OpenLibrary() function. Since each process has its own library pointer all socket descriptors are private to each process. Passing on socket descriptors between different processes is not supported and each process will have its own limit on the number of sockets it can have open at the same time.

A socket can be 'blocking' or it can be set to 'non-blocking' operation. When a socket is blocking then any function that uses it may block execution (make the program wait) until the function has finished. For example a call to connect() may not return until the connection has been made or an error has occurred. This makes for easy straightforward programming since the return value of connect() will show if the connection is there or not. But at the same time the program will sit there without responding to user input and the user may wonder if it has crashed.

With a non-blocking socket all functions will return immediately but the actual function may not (yet) have been performed. Calling connect() on a non-blocking socket may return an error or an 'in progress' indication. The connection has not (yet) been established and of course can still fail.

The program therefore needs to continue to check if the connection has been established or if this has failed. This is more work for the programmer compared to the blocking socket, but results in a program that can still respond to the user. To make this a bit easier the Amiga network stack offers an asynchronous events system that allows programs to stay informed about the status of its sockets while also dealing with other events and messages, like for example Intuition messages.

When programs are run from the CLI/shell then the bsdsocket.library allows its functions to be interrupted by the user performing a break. By default the break action expected by the bsdsocket.library is set to Ctrl+C. When a user break happens then the SIGBREAKF_CTRL_C signal of the process will be set to indicate this.

Addressing

The previous chapters have shown that IP connections require an address and a port number. The bsdsocket.library provides a number of functions that help with conversion of addresses as well as resolving domain names into addresses in order to use them for communication. This section will detail some of these functions as well as the structs used.

The following headers are needed for these functions: sys/socket.h, netinet/in.h and arpa/inet.h.

inet_addr

Convert an IP address string into a binary address.

```
unsigned long address = inet_addr( char * cp );
                D0                          A0
```

cp - A null-terminated string containing an IP address in dot notation.

When conversion of the address was successful the function will return the resulting binary address. If the address string is invalid then the function will return the INADDR_NONE value.

Inet_NtoA

Convert a binary address into a string.

```
char * result = Inet_NtoA( unsigned long in );
         D0                              D0
```

in – An Internet address in 32 bits binary format.

The binary address is converted to a character string for which the result is returned as a pointer. This function will always succeed. The location for the result string is statically allocated and will be overwritten with subsequent calls.

gethostbyname

Get a host's address by resolving its name.

```
struct hostent * he = gethostbyname( char * name );
                 D0                              A0
```

name - A pointer to a null-terminated string with the name to resolve.

This function will return a pointer to the hostent struct with the resulting information or NULL in case of an error. Use the *h_errno* variable to find out what the error was. The returned pointer will point at a static data location, which will be overwritten each time this function is called.

The hostent structure contains the following fields:

```
struct hostent {
    char *  h_name;         // Pointer to a string with the official name of the host
    char ** h_aliases;      // Pointer to an array with other names of the host
    long    h_addrtype;     // Type of address, always AF_INET for the Amiga
    long    h_length;       // The length in bytes of each address
    char ** h_addr_list;    // Pointer to an array of addresses for the host
};
```

h_name - Points at a string with the host's official name. When a system has multiple names this could be a different name than the one used for the query.

h_aliases - Points to a zero terminated array of names for hosts with multiple names.

h_length - The number of bytes used by an address. For an IPv4 address this number is 4.

h_addr_list - A zero terminated array of addresses for the host. There should always be at least one address in the array but more could be in the list for hosts that have multiple addresses.

For backward compatibility there is a macro called h_addr, which translates into h_addr_list[0] and is used to access the first address in the array.

Setting up sockets

A socket is an endpoint that sends and/or receives data. The bsdsocket.library has an internal table where it maintains the sockets and the status of each of them. When a socket is created the library passes on the table index of the socket. This index is the socket descriptor and is used by all socket related functions.

Since each application that opens the library gets its own library base it also gets its own socket table. It is therefore not possible to pass on socket descriptors between different applications.

The following headers are needed for these functions: sys/types.h and sys/socket.h.

socket

Create a socket to use for communication.

```
long result = socket( long domain, long type, long protocol );
     D0                      D0         D1         D2
```

domain - The domain selects the suite of protocols that can be used. On current Amiga network stacks only AF_INET is supported, which selects the ARPA Internet protocols.

type - The type of socket to be used. This also defines which IP protocol is being used.

protocol - For selecting a particular protocol to be used. Since each type only supports one protocol the value is always 0.

The function will try to create a socket and return the socket descriptor when successful. It will return -1 when unsuccessful, the reason for the failure can be read from the *errno* variable.

The following types are supported:

> SOCK_STREAM - Use the socket with TCP connections.
>
> SOCK_DGRAM - Use the socket with UDP datagrams.
>
> SOCK_RAW - Use the socket to access the raw network protocol. Useful for ICMP.

CloseSocket

Close a socket and free its resources.

```
long result = CloseSocket( long sd );
     D0                         D0
```

sd - The socket descriptor of the socket to close. The socket descriptor is usually obtained from the socket() function or the accept() function.

The function will try to close the socket and free any resources used by it. When successful the function will return 0. If not successful it will return -1 and the reason for the failure can be found by checking the *errno* variable.

By default the CloseSocket() function will close the connection and free all resources. This may cause any unsent data still residing in the internal buffer to be lost. It is possible to change this behaviour for SOCK_STREAM sockets with the SO_LINGER option of the setsockopt() function. This option allows for setting a 'linger' time during which the network stack continues to attempt to send the data in the internal buffer. If the data was sent successfully while lingering CloseSocket() will return as soon as the data is sent and return 0. Otherwise CloseSocket() will return after the linger time has expired and return -1.

Each process has its own library base, which means that calling Exec's CloseLibrary() on the bsdsocket.library pointer allows the library to automatically close all sockets owned by the process. However, each process also has a limit on the number of sockets that can be open at the same time and keeping unused sockets open may cause the process to run out of sockets. Closing the library while sockets are not closed may also lead to loss of data in the internal buffers as no lingering will be performed. For these reasons calling CloseSocket() on a socket that is no longer needed is always good practice.

Connections

For TCP based communication there are two sides to a connection. The host that creates the connection by calling connect() has the active connection, while the host that received the connection by calling accept() has the passive connection. The term active or passive only depends on which side made the connection and does not depend on the direction of the data flow. As an example, a web browser makes an active connection to the web server and the web server has a passive connection with this browser. Even though the main flow of data is from server to browser.

While UDP based communication does not have a connection on the protocol level, some of these functions can be used for UDP as well.

The following headers are needed for these functions: sys/types.h and sys/socket.h.

connect

Start a connection on a socket.

```
long success = connect( long sd, struct sockaddr * addr, long addrlen );
        D0                    D0                      A0          D1
```

sd - The socket descriptor of the socket to use for the connection.

addr - Pointer to a sockaddr structure with the address and port of the destination.

addrlen - Length of the sockaddr structure.

The function will return a 0 on success and -1 if there is a failure or if the socket is non-blocking. The reason for returning -1 can be found in the *errno* variable, which in the case of a non-blocking socket could be set to EINPROGRESS, meaning that the connection process is still under way. On a blocking socket this function will block until either the connection has been established, or the creation of it has failed.

For SOCK_STREAM type of sockets this function will start the process of connecting to the destination of which the address and port are provided via the *addr* argument. If the socket is already connected then the EISCONN error will be generated.

For SOCK_DGRAM sockets this function will associate the socket with the destination address. This means that all datagrams sent with the send() function will be addressed to the destination and only datagrams coming from the destination will be received; datagrams from other destinations will be dropped on this socket. To remove an associated destination call connect() with a null address in the sockaddr struct.

The sockaddr structure is not tied to a particular address format. This is since the standard BSD implementation of connect() can be used with sockets that connect over networks that use protocols and addressing schemes that are very different from the way the Internet protocols do things. For each of these protocols there is a different sockaddr struct. The Amiga network stacks only supports IP connectivity and as such only the Internet version of the sockaddr structure is supported, which is named sockaddr_in. It contains the following fields:

```
struct sockaddr_in {
    short           sin_family;     // Always AF_INET
    u_short         sin_port;       // Port number
    struct in_addr  sin_addr;       // IP address in binary form
    char            sin_zero[8];    // Unused
};
```

sin_family - This field is used to differentiate the various versions of the sockaddr struct. For sockaddr_in this field must be set to AF_INET.

sin_port - The port number to connect to on the destination host.

sin_addr - The address to connect to in binary notation. The in_addr struct contains only a single long named s_addr, which stores the actual address bytes.

bind

Associate a socket with a local address and port.

```
long success = bind( long sd, struct sockaddr * addr, long addrlen );
          D0             D0                     A0           D1
```

sd - Descriptor of the socket.

addr - Pointer to a sockaddr structure with the address and port number to bind to.

addrlen - Length of the *addr* sockaddr structure.

A call to bind() will return 0 on success and -1 if there was a failure. The type of failure can be found from the *errno* variable.

For Internet use the sockaddr struct again is a sockaddr_in struct (see the connect() function) with its pointer cast to the generic sockaddr struct. Where the sockaddr_in for the connect() function contained the address and port of the remote host, for the bind() function they contain a local address and port to bind the socket to.

When a socket is created it will be assigned a random port number, also known as the ephemeral port number. This is fine for outgoing connections but for incoming connections the socket usually needs to be on a predetermined 'known' port number. The bind() function is used to bind the socket to a specific port number. An example of this is a web server, which usually binds to port 80 for its clear text connections and port 443 for its secure connections.

The bind() function can also be used to bind a socket to a particular local address, which is useful on systems with multiple interfaces where the socket needs to respond only to a particular interface. For example, binding to the local loopback address (127.0.0.1) means that the socket is limited to connections from the host itself. If there is no need to limit the socket to a particular address the value of INADDR_ANY can be used for the address. Using INADDR_ANY will result in the socket being bound to the port on all addresses on this system.

If there already is another socket of the same type bound to the port and address then bind() will fail. The SOCK_STREAM type and SOCK_DGRAM type sockets are completely separate entities. It is therefore absolutely fine to bind a SOCK_DGRAM socket as well as a SOCK_STREAM socket using the same address and port.

listen

Prepare a socket for incoming connections.

```
long success = listen( long sd, long backlog );
        D0                    D0        D1
```

sd - The descriptor of the socket to receive connections on.

backlog - The size of the queue of incoming connections.

The function sets the socket up to listen for incoming connections and is only supported by SOCK_STREAM type sockets. Incoming connections will be placed in a queue and can be established one by one by calling accept(). The *backlog* argument defines the size of the queue and incoming connections arriving while the queue is full may be rejected by the network stack. The listen() function will return a 0 on success and -1 if there was a failure. The type of failure can be found from the *errno* variable.

accept

Accept an incoming connection on a socket.

```
long sd = accept( long sd, struct sockaddr * addr, long * addrlen );
     D0                 D0                          A0            A1
```

sd - Descriptor of a socket that was prepared for incoming connections with a call to listen().

addr - Pointer to a sockaddr struct that will be filled with the address details of the remote host that is connecting.

addrlen - Pointer to a long that initially will hold the size of the space used by the sockaddr struct. When accept() returns successfully the long will contain the actual size of the sockaddr struct that was returned.

The function will get the first connection request from the queue and return a new socket descriptor for the connection. If the queue is empty and the socket is blocking then the function will not return until there is an incoming connection. If there is an error then the function will return -1 and the *errno* variable will hold the reason. If the socket is non-blocking and there are no connection requests in the queue then accept() will return -1 with *errno* set to EWOULDBLOCK.

The socket that was used for the *sd* argument is left unchanged and can therefore be used to accept further incoming connections. Each newly accepted connection will result in a new socket being created for the new connection. If no more incoming connections will be accepted then the socket can be closed with a call to CloseSocket(). This will not affect the new sockets that were created for the accepted connections.

The new socket returned by accept() will have the same properties as the listening socket. If, for example, the listening socket is non-blocking then the socket returned will be non-blocking as well. The new socket can only be used for the established connection and cannot be used to accept further incoming connections. When a connection is finished the socket can be closed with a call to CloseSocket(), which will not affect any other accepted connection, nor will it affect the original listening socket.

shutdown

Start the shutdown process on a TCP connection.

```
long success = shutdown( long sd, long how );
     D0                       D0        D1
```

sd - Descriptor of the socket with the connection.

how – Value defining how the shutdown process is started.

When shutdown() is successful it will return a zero, otherwise the value -1 will be returned and the reason for the error can be found in the *errno* value.

The *how* argument can have one of the following values:

> 0 - Shutdown receiving on the connection.

> 1 - Shutdown sending on the connection.

> 2 - Shutdown receiving as well as sending on the connection.

With this function the connection can be terminated in a controlled fashion, or even in stages. Calling CloseSocket() on a connected socket will immediately destroy the connection and free the socket descriptor. Any unread or unsent data in the internal buffers will be lost.

Using shutdown() a host can indicate that no more data will be sent by calling the function with a value of 1 for the *how* argument. The other host will receive all data that was sent up to this point and then receive an EOF (End-Of-File) indication. When the other host is also done sending it can call its own shutdown() function with a *how* value of 1. When both hosts have received the EOF indication all data has been transferred and none has been lost. Both hosts can now safely call the CloseSocket() function to free the socket.

Transferring data

During data transfer it is important to keep the difference between UDP and TCP in mind since this will also affect how data is received from the socket.

With TCP the received data will be copied into the internal receive buffer. The data will be in the same order as it was sent and there will be no duplicate data or missing data. The receive functions will copy the data from the internal buffer without any correlation to how the data was packaged into the different segments when it was received.

For UDP the received data is also copied into the internal receive buffer, but the data from different datagrams will be kept apart from each other. The data in the buffer will be in the same order as the datagrams were received, which may not be the same order as they were sent in and the buffer may also include duplicates. The receive functions can only read one datagram worth of data per call and will read these in the order they are buffered. There is no indication of how many datagrams may have been missed.

The following headers are needed for these functions: sys/types.h and sys/socket.h.

send

Send data over a socket.

```
long result = send( long sd, void * data, long datalen, long flags );
      D0                      D0          A0           D1              D2
```

sd - Descriptor of the socket to use.

data - Pointer to a block of data to be sent.

datalen - Length of the data (in bytes) to be sent.

flags - A number of bits for selecting specific behaviour or options.

The result of the function will indicate the number of bytes copied into the internal buffer or -1 when a failure is detected. The *errno* variable will contain the reason for the failure. Please note that send() indicating that any or all *datalen* bytes were copied does not guarantee that the remote host will also have received them successfully.

If send() is called on a blocking socket and there is no space in the internal buffer of the network stack then the function will block until there is space in the buffer. If the socket is non-blocking and the internal buffer is full then the function will return immediately with a value of -1 and *errno* set to EAGAIN. If there is space in the buffer then send() will copy the data into the internal buffer and return immediately, it does this for blocking sockets as well as non-blocking sockets. Importantly, even for blocking sockets it does not wait for the data to be received and acknowledged by the remote host.

For active TCP connections (socket type SOCK_STREAM) the socket must previously have been used for a call to connect() and the connection must have been established. For passive TCP connections the socket must be one that was returned by a call to accept().

The send() function can also be used to transmit UDP datagrams (socket type SOCK_DGRAM) but only for sockets that have been used with a call to connect() to set the address and port number of the destination host.

The following *flags* are supported:

MSG_OOB - Send data out-of-band (SOCK_STREAM type only).

MSG_DONTROUTE - Ignore the routing table (usually only used by routing software).

sendto

Send a datagram over a socket.

```
long result = sendto( long sd, void * msg, long len, long flags,
    D0                    D0        A0       D1        D2
                                            struct sockaddr * to, long tolen );
                                                              A1        D3
```

sd - Descriptor of the socket to use.

msg - Pointer to the data to send.

len - Length of the data in bytes.

flags - A number of bits for selecting specific behaviour or options.

to - Pointer to a sockaddr structure with the address and port number of the destination.

tolen - Length of the sockaddr structure used for the *to* argument.

The result of the function will indicate the number of bytes copied into the internal buffer or -1 when a failure is detected. The *errno* variable will contain the reason for the failure. Please note that sendto() indicating success does not guarantee that the remote host will also have received the datagram.

If sendto() is called on a blocking socket and there is no space in the internal buffer of the network stack then the function will block until there is space in the buffer. If the socket is non-blocking and the internal buffer is full then the function will return immediately with a value of -1 and *errno* set to EAGAIN. If there is enough space in the buffer then sendto() will copy the data to the internal buffer and return immediately, for blocking sockets as well as non-blocking sockets.

The socket used for sendto() does not need to have been used for a call to connect().

If sendto() is called with a NULL value for the *to* argument then the function will respond exactly like send() does. In that case a prior call to connect() is required. With a NULL value for the *to* argument it is also possible to use sendto() with SOCK_STREAM type sockets.

The following *flags* are supported:

MSG_OOB - Send data out-of-band (SOCK_STREAM type only).

MSG_DONTROUTE - Ignore the routing table (usually only used by routing software).

recv

Receive data over a socket.

```
long result = recv( long sd, void * buf, long buflen, long flags );
     D0                    D0         A0         D1          D2
```

sd - Descriptor of the socket to use.

buf - Pointer to a buffer into which the received data will be copied.

buflen - Size of the buffer (in bytes).

flags - A number of bits for selecting specific behaviour or options.

The result of the function will indicate the number of bytes copied into *buf* or -1 when a failure is detected. The *errno* variable will contain the reason for the failure. If there is more data than fits the buffer and the socket is of SOCK_STREAM type then only the data that fits will be copied into the buffer. The rest of the data can be retrieved with a subsequent call to recv(). If the socket is of type SOCK_DGRAM and the data is larger than *buflen* bytes then only *buflen* bytes will be copied and the rest of the datagram will be discarded.

If recv() is called on a blocking socket while there is no received data then the socket will block until data has been received. If the socket is non-blocking then recv() will return -1 if there is no data and *errno* will be set to EAGAIN. If there is any received data then the function will copy the data to the buffer and return the number of bytes copied. The function will not wait until *buflen* number of bytes are received; the amount of data copied can therefore be any size up to *buflen*.

A value of zero is returned by recv() when an EOF occurs. This is usually caused by the remote host calling shutdown() on the socket with either a value of 1 or a value of 2 for the *how* argument. After this it is safe to assume that no more data will be received.

The socket that is used for recv() must already be part of a connection. For SOCK_STREAM type sockets this socket must have been used with connect() (and the connection has been established) or for incoming connections it must be a socket returned by accept(). The recv() function can also be used to receive UDP datagrams but connect() must have been called on the socket first.

The following *flags* are supported:

> MSG_OOB - Receive data out-of-band (SOCK_STREAM type only).

> MSG_PEEK - Copy received data to the buffer, but leave it in the queue.

> MSG_WAITALL - Block until all *buflen* bytes have been received. The function will still return on error, disconnect or sigbreak.

recvfrom

Receive a datagram over a socket.

```
long result = recvfrom( long sd, void * buf, long buflen, long flags,
     D0                      D0          A0          D1           D2
                                    struct sockaddr * from, long * fromlen );
                                                      A1            A2
```

sd - Descriptor of the socket to use.

buf - Pointer to a buffer into which the received data will be copied.

buflen - Size of the buffer (in bytes).

flags - A number of bits for selecting specific behaviour or options.

from - Pointer to a sockaddr struct that will be filled with the address details of the remote host that sent the datagram.

fromlen - Pointer to a long that initially will hold the size of the space used by the *from* sockaddr struct. When recvfrom() returns successfully the long will contain the actual size of the sockaddr struct that was returned.

The result of the function will indicate the number of bytes copied into the buffer or -1 when a failure has occurred. The *errno* variable will contain the reason for the failure. The sockaddr struct pointed to by the *from* argument will contain the address and port of the host the data originated from. The long pointed at by the *fromlen* variable will contain the length of the sockaddr_in struct.

If there is more data than fits the buffer and the socket is of SOCK_STREAM type then only the data that fits will be copied into the buffer. The rest of the data can be retrieved with a subsequent call. If the socket is of type SOCK_DGRAM and the data is larger than *buflen* bytes then only *buflen* bytes will be copied and the rest of the datagram will be discarded.

If recvfrom() is called on a blocking socket while there is no received data then the socket will block until data has been received. If the socket is non-blocking then recvfrom() will return -1 if there is no data and *errno* will be set to EAGAIN. If there is data then the function will copy the data to the buffer and return the number of bytes copied. The function will not wait until *buflen* number of bytes are received; the amount of data copied can therefore be any size up to *buflen*.

A value of zero is returned by recvfrom() when an EOF occurs. This is usually caused by the remote host calling shutdown() on the socket with either a value of 1 or a value of 2 for the *how* argument. After this it is safe to assume that no more data will be received.

If recvfrom() is called with a NULL value for the *from* argument then the function will respond exactly like recv() does. In this case a prior call to connect() is required. With a NULL value for the *from* argument it is also possible to use recvfrom() with SOCK_STREAM type sockets.

The following *flags* are supported:

> MSG_OOB - Receive data out-of-band (SOCK_STREAM type only).

> MSG_PEEK - Copy received data to the buffer, but leave it in the queue.

> MSG_WAITALL - Block until all *buflen* bytes have been received. The function will still return on error, disconnect or sigbreak.

Configuration

The library offers a number of functions that allow an application to change the way its sockets behave. This includes changing the socket between blocking and non-blocking, setting lower level protocol parameters like the TTL and specifying the signal masks for sigbreak as well as asynchronous event signalling.

The following headers are needed for these functions: libraries/bsdsocket.h, sys/types.h, sys/socket.h and sys/ioctl.h.

IoctlSocket

Access a socket's I/O parameters.

```
long result = IoctlSocket( long sd, unsigned long request, char * argp );
        D0                      D0              D1            A0
```

sd - Descriptor of the socket of which to access a parameter.

request - Identifies the parameter and the type of access required.

argp - Pointer to the argument of the request, the type of which depends on the *request* value.

When an error occurs the function will set the *errno* value and return -1.

Some of the requests supported:

> FIONBIO - Enable/disable non-blocking mode on the socket. The *argp* pointer must point to a long. When this long has a value of 1 the socket will be non-blocking, if the value is 0 then the socket will be in blocking mode.

FIOASYNC - Enable/disable asynchronous events on the socket. The *argp* pointer must point to a long. When this long has a value of 1 the socket's asynchronous events will be enabled, if the value is 0 then the socket will not generate any asynchronous events.

FIONREAD - Return the number of bytes available to read on the socket. The *argp* pointer must point to a long, this long will receive the number of bytes available for reading.

setsockopt

Set options on a socket.

```
long result = setsockopt( long sd, long level, long optname,
       D0                      D0       D1        D2
                                                   void * optval, long optlen );
                                                     A0                D3
```

sd - Descriptor of the socket of which to set the option.

level - Level at which the option is to be set.

optname - The name of the option that needs to be set.

optval - A pointer to the new value for the option.

optlen - The length in bytes of the value pointed to by the *optval* argument.

The setsockopt() function will return a 0 on success and a -1 on failure. The reason for the failure can be found in the *errno* variable.

Some of the *levels* supported:

SOL_SOCKET - The option is for the socket itself. The option name starts with SO.

IPPROTO_IP - The option is for the IP header part of the protocol. The option name starts with IP.

IPPROTO_TCP - The option is for the TCP protocol and is supported by SOCK_STREAM type sockets only. The option name starts with TCP.

IPPROTO_UDP - The option is for the UDP protocol and is supported by SOCK_DGRAM type sockets only. The option name starts with UDP.

Some of the *optname* values supported:

SO_EVENTMASK – Select the asynchronous events the socket should generate. Please read the description of the GetSocketEvents() function for the supported events. The *optval* argument should point at a ULONG of the selected events bitwise OR-ed together.

SO_LINGER – Block on CloseSocket() if the socket is of SOCK_STREAM type and there is still data present in the internal buffers. When lingering is enabled the CloseSocket() call will block until all data is sent or until the linger time has passed. The *optval* argument should point at a linger structure, which looks as follows:

```
struct linger {
  LONG    l_onoff;    // Set to 0 to turn off lingering, set to 1 to turn it on.
  LONG    l_linger;   // Maximum linger time in seconds.
};
```

TCP_NODELAY – Disable the Nagle algorithm so that data is always sent out immediately. The *optval* argument should point at an integer variable set to a non-zero value to enable the option (which disables the Nagle algorithm) or set to zero to disable the option (and enable the Nagle algorithm again).

TCP_MAXSEG – Set the maximum segment size allowed.

IP_TTL – Set the time-to-live value in the IP header of the packets being sent. This does not affect the TTL value of multicast datagrams.

IP_TOS - Set the type-of-service value in the IP header of the packets being sent.

IP_MULTICAST_TTL – Specify the time-to-live value used in the IP header of any multicast datagrams that are being sent. This does not affect the TTL value of non-multicast packets.

IP_MULTICAST_LOOP – When an application is transmitting to a multicast group and is also receiving from the same group then the data will by default also be looped back to the application so that it receives its own data. This option allows the loop to be disabled by using a 32 bits value of zero. Using a non-zero value will enable the looping of data again. Disabling looping will also mean that multiple instances on the same host will not be able to see each other's transmissions.

IP_ADD_MEMBERSHIP – Join a multicast group in order to receive the data that is sent to it. The *optval* argument should point at an ip_mreq structure, which looks as follows:

```
struct ip_mreq {
    struct in_addr imr_multiaddr; // The multicast address of the group to join.
    struct in_addr imr_interface; // The interface address (usually INADDR_ANY).
};
```

IP_DROP_MEMBERSHIP – Leave a multicast group. The *optval* argument should point at an ip_mreq structure (shown above).

getsockopt

Get the current value of an option on a socket.

```
long result = getsockopt( long sd, long level, long optname,
    D0                        D0        D1         D2
                                        void * optval, long * optlen );
                                             A0              A1
```

sd - Descriptor of the socket from which to get the option.

level - Level of the option to get (see setsockopt()).

optname - The name of the option to get.

optval - A pointer to a location where getsockopt() can store the current value for the option.

optlen - A pointer to a long that initially contains the byte size of the storage space pointed to by the *optval* argument. When the function returns successfully the long pointed to by *optlen* will contain the actual size of the data stored in the *optval* storage space.

The function will return a 0 on success and a -1 on failure. The reason for the failure can be found in the *errno* variable.

The getsockopt() function supports the same options as setsockopt(). There are also a number of SOL_SOCKET options that are read-only and therefore only supported by getsockopt():

> SO_TYPE - Get the socket's type (for example SOCK_STREAM or SOCK_DGRAM).

> SO_ERROR - Get the current error value (if any) and clear it.

SocketBaseTagList

Access socket library base parameters.

```
long result = SocketBaseTags( Tag first, ... );
long result = SocketBaseTagList( struct TagItem * tags );
    D0                                            A0
```

tags - Standard Amiga style tag list with each tag identifying the parameter to read or change.

This function returns a 0 on success and a positive number on error. This positive number is the index of the tag that failed, with the first tag in the list having an index of one.

There are two versions of the function. The SocketBaseTagList() version takes a pointer to an array with the tags, the last tag in the array being TAG_END. The SocketBaseTags() function takes all tags as a list of arguments, where the last argument must always be TAG_END.

The tags used in the list are created by combining the name of the parameter with the required operation and the type of argument. The parameter names all start with SBTC_ (which stands for 'Socket Base Tag Code') and one of the following operations:

SBTF_GET - Get the current value of a parameter.

SBTF_SET - Set a new value for the parameter.

And one of the following argument types can be used:

SBTF_VAL - The argument value is stored directly in the taglist.

SBTF_REF - A pointer to the argument value is stored in the taglist.

From this list each tag must be either a GET or a SET and must be either be a VAL or a REF. From all this the formula for creating the actual TAG name is as follows:

Name = TAG_USER | (operation) | (argument type) | parameter name << 1) ;

This formula is mostly required by assembly programs since for C programming the SDK provides four macros that only require the parameter name to be specified and then add the other values depending on the macro chosen:

SBTM_GETREF(parameter name) - Get the parameter's current value and use the pointer in the argument to store the value.

SBTM_GETVAL(parameter name) - Get the parameter's current value and store it in the argument in the tag list.

SBTM_SETREF(parameter name) - Set the parameter's new value by using the pointer in the argument to get the new value.

SBTM_SETVAL(parameter name) - Set the parameter's new value directly from the argument in the tag list.

Some of the supported parameters:

SBTC_DTABLESIZE - The maximum number of sockets in the descriptor table. This defines the maximum number of sockets that the program can open.

SBTC_ERRNO - The current value of the *errno* variable.

SBTC_ERRNOLONGPTR - The pointer to the *errno* variable. This for example allows a program to set its own variable for the bsdsocket.library to use.

SBTC_ERRNOSTRPTR - Get the pointer to a human readable error message string for a particular *errno* code. When calling provide a pointer to a long with the *errno* value. On return the function will have changed this to a pointer to the matching error string.

SBTC_HERRNO - The current value of the *h_errno* variable. This variable is a long.

SBTC_HERRNOSTRPTR - Get the pointer to a human readable error message string for a particular *h_errno* code. When calling provide a pointer to a long with the *h_errno* value. On return the function will have changed this to a pointer to the matching error string.

SBTC_BREAKMASK - Set the mask of the Exec signal to be used as a user break event. By default this is SIGBREAKF_CTRL_C. This is only used by programs running from the CLI/Shell. Programs started from Workbench will not receive any SIGBREAKF_ signals.

SBTC_SIGEVENTMASK - Set the mask of the Exec signal used for asynchronous events.

Socket status

In any multitasking operating system like AmigaOS it is important to not waste CPU power on polling loops but to use the OS to sleep the process until something happens that the program needs to respond to. These functions help to setup that kind of processing.

The WaitSelect() function is the Amiga version of the BSD select() function and can be used to wait as well as find out what the status of multiple sockets is.

The GetSocketEvents() function is an Amiga specific function that can be used together with Exec signals to find out which event(s) on which socket caused the process to be woken up.

The following headers are needed for these functions: sys/types.h, sys/time.h and exec/types.h.

WaitSelect

Wait for a socket's event to occur.

```
long Result = WaitSelect( long nfds, fd_set * readfds, fd_set * writefds,
   D0                       D0            A0              A1
            fd_set * exceptfds, struct timeval * timeout, ULONG * signals );
                  A2                    A3              D1
```

nfds - The number of socket descriptors to test in each list.

readfds - Pointer to a socket descriptor set to be tested if they are ready for reading or NULL.

writefds - Pointer to a socket descriptor set to be tested if they are ready for writing or NULL.

exceptfds - Pointer to a socket descriptor set to be tested for exceptions or NULL.

timeout - Maximum time to wait for events to occur. Set to NULL to never timeout.

signals - Pointing to a mask of Exec signals that should interrupt WaitSelect(). Set to NULL if this functionality is not required.

WaitSelect() will return the number of tested descriptors that have found to be ready (or had an exception). The function will return 0 if a timeout occurred and -1 if there was an error or if the function got interrupted by a signal. When the function returns -1 the reason can be found in the *errno* variable.

To make it possible for the function to check multiple sockets at the same time it makes use of descriptor sets rather than single descriptor values. If a particular state does not need to be tested then a NULL can be passed instead of a pointer to a set. For example, if no sockets need to be tested for write readiness then a NULL can be passed for the *writefds* argument. The sets are used as input as well as output. When calling the function each set will contain the sockets to be tested. When the function returns it will have modified the descriptor sets to include only the descriptors of the sockets that are ready. If the function returns -1 the sets will not have been modified.

A number of C macros are provided for dealing with the socket descriptor sets:

FD_ZERO(fd_set * fdset) - Initialise the set as an empty set.

FD_SET(long sd, fd_set * fdset) - Add a socket descriptor to the set.

FD_CLR(long sd, fd_set * fdset) - Remove a socket descriptor from the set.

FD_ISSET(long sd, fd_set * fdset) - Test if a socket descriptor is present in the set.

The *nfds* argument specifies the number of descriptors to be tested in each set. For example, if each set contains seven descriptors and the *nfds* argument is set to three then only the first three descriptors will be tested, the other four will be ignored. As a result on return of the function only the state of the three tested sockets should be relied upon; the result of the four untested sockets will be undefined.

The *timeout* argument takes a pointer to a timeval structure. This structure is defined by AmigaOS in devices/timer.h. There is a slight difference between this structure and the one expected by socket implementations. With some compilers this causes a compiler warning that can be safely ignored. The AmigaOS version of the struct looks as follows:

```
struct timeval {
    ULONG   tv_secs;      // Number of seconds, must be smaller than 100000000.
    ULONG   tv_micro;     // Number of micro seconds, must be smaller than 1000000.
};
```

To make WaitSelect() update the descriptor sets and return immediately set both members of the timeval struct to 0. To make WaitSelect() never time out pass a NULL for the *timeout* argument.

The *signals* argument is a pointer to a ULONG with a mask of Exec signals that WaitSelect() should return on. When the function returns with a value of zero or more then the mask in the ULONG will have been replaced with a mask of the signals that have been received. If WaitSelect() returns a -1 then the ULONG will not have been modified. If no user signals are needed then a NULL can be passed. If a user break signal is being used then there is no need to add this to the signal mask; the network stack will already deal with this internally and the function will return -1 with an appropriate code in *errno* even when NULL is passed for the signals argument.

Please note that this function requires a lot of stack to perform. The autodocs speak of "several thousands of bytes" for each time the function is called. The function may also need to allocate additional memory, which will make the call take extra time.

GetSocketEvents

Get the next asynchronous event generated by the socket.

```
long sd = GetSocketEvents( ULONG * events_ptr );
     D0                              A0
```

events_ptr - Pointer to a ULONG which will receive the pending events for a socket.

The function will return -1 if no events have occurred. Otherwise the function will return the socket descriptor of the socket for which one or more events occurred and place a bit mask of the events in the ULONG pointed to by *events_ptr*. The reason for using a mask is that more than one event may have occurred for the socket since the last call to GetSocketEvents().

The following events are supported:

> FD_CONNECT - An outgoing connection has been established successfully. This event is generated by non-blocking SOCK_STREAM type sockets. Blocking sockets may not generate this event on all networking stacks since on success the connection will already have been established when connect() returned.

> FD_ACCEPT - An incoming connection is ready to be accepted. Only for SOCK_STREAM type sockets that have had listen() called on them. In the case of multiple incoming connections an FD_ACCEPT event will be generated for each individual connection.

FD_READ - Data has been received and can be read with one of the recv() functions. This event can be generated by all types of socket and includes blocking as well as non-blocking operation. On some network stacks receiving the FD_CLOSE event will stop any further FD_READ events from being generated, even if there is still data to be read from the internal buffer.

FD_WRITE - There is space in the internal buffers for sending. This event can be generated by all types of socket and includes blocking as well as non-blocking operation. On some network stacks this message will only be generated after the first call to send().

FD_CLOSE - The connection on the socket has been closed. This event will be signalled directly when the connection is closed by the remote host, even when there still is unread data in the internal buffers of the network stack. It is up to the program to ensure that the rest of the data is read before calling CloseSocket() on the socket.

FD_ERROR - An error occurred. The error may not always be set in the *errno* variable. When *errno* is not set then the actual error code needs to be read from the socket using the getsockopt() function with the SOL_SOCKET and SO_ERROR arguments.

FD_OOB - There is out-of-band data available for receiving.

5. Sockets in C

This chapter goes into the practical side of using the bsdsocket.library in programs written in C. There are two TCP based examples, one that shows how to make a connection to a server and one that acts as a server and receives connections. The UDP example shows how datagrams can be sent as well as received, while the multicast example does the same but adds the joining and leaving of the multicast group.

For brevity the code shown here has most of the error recovery removed, the full source in the download will have most of this implemented. There will be small differences between the code here in the book and the code in the sources; this is done for brevity, although the full source code in the downloads will receive irregular updates as well.

All these examples are meant to be run from the CLI/Shell and not from the Workbench. This is mainly since it allows the examples use the CLI/Shell window to show status by using printf().

Setting up

There is a small amount of preparation to be done before the socket can be opened and used for communication. Most of the preparation done is to setup AmigaOS and to setup communication with the socket library.

When using the GCC compiler the bsdsocket.library needs to be opened before use and closed again before terminating the program. Due to the use of the -lauto linker flag there is no need to open and close the bsdsocket.library when using the VBCC compiler.

The header files for the Roadshow network stack can be found in the "SANA+RoadshowTCP-IP" directory that is part of the AmigaOS 3.2 NDK. These header files are compatible with other Amiga network stacks as well; using these headers does not mean that the program will only work with the Roadshow network stack but it will be also be compatible with other TCP/IP networking stacks for the Amiga.

Increasing the stack size

The default stack size used by AmigaOS is not large enough for some of the functions of the bsdsocket.library. This can lead to the program overrunning the stack, which can in turn cause odd crashes and system reboots.

The amount of stack required by a program can be specified via the 'stack cookie', which is a string embedded in the program that informs the OS of the amount of stack required. For VBCC this is done as follows:

```
__entry char StackCookie[] = "$STACK:10240";
```

The '__entry' keyword is used to tell VBCC that the string is not used in the code but should not be removed by the optimiser. Other compilers will need a different keyword, for example the GCC compiler uses '__attribute__((used))' instead:

```
__attribute__((used)) char StackCookie[] = "$STACK:10240";
```

Signals and error codes

The BSD socket interface uses two variables to store error codes in, *errno* and *h_errno*. The bsdsocket.library needs a pointer to these variables in order to be able to access them. This is done via the SocketBaseTags() function. A signal also needs to be allocated so that the library can use it for signalling asynchronous events. This can be done during the same call to SocketBaseTags(). The Exec function AllocSignal() allocates a free signal and returns the bit number of the signal. This bit number is then converted to a bitmask for the SocketBaseTags() function:

```
ULONG ErrNo=0;
ULONG HErrNo=0;

BYTE SocketSignal = AllocSignal( -1 );
ULONG SocketSignalMask = 1 << SocketSignal;

SocketBaseTags( SBTM_SETVAL(SBTC_ERRNOLONGPTR), &ErrNo,
        SBTM_SETVAL(SBTC_HERRNOLONGPTR), &HErrNo,
        SBTM_SETVAL(SBTC_SIGEVENTMASK), SocketSignalMask,
        TAG_END );
```

The *ErrNo* and *HErrNo* variables are used as global variables so that other functions can have access to them as well. For non-blocking sockets various socket functions may return -1 to indicate an ongoing state instead of an error. This requires the *ErrNo* variable to be accessible so it can be checked to see if the -1 return was a genuine error or not.

Getting error code information

When the socket functions indicate that an error has occurred the code that describes the error can be found in the *ErrNo* variable (or the *HErrNo* variable for a small number of functions). The socket library also provides a method to convert the *ErrNo* code into a human readable string. This is done by calling SocketBaseTagList() with SBTM_GETVAL(SBTC_ERRNOSTRPTR) as one of the tags in the list. The data field for the tag is filled with the code of the *ErrNo* variable.

The SocketBaseTagList() function is then called with the taglist as its argument. When the function returns successfully it will have replaced the error code in the tag's data field with a pointer to the human readable string with the error description.

```
struct TagItem tags[2];
tags[0].ti_Tag  = SBTM_GETVAL(SBTC_ERRNOSTRPTR);
tags[0].ti_Data = Error;    // The error code to be converted into a string
tags[1].ti_Tag  = TAG_END;  // Signal the end of the taglist

if ( SocketBaseTagList( tags ) != 0 )
{
    printf( "%s Unkown error: %ld\n", pMsg, ErrNo );
}
else
{
    char * pErrStr = (char *)tags[0].ti_Data;
    printf( "%s Error: %ld (%s)\n", pMsg, ErrNo, pErrStr );
}
```

This function can also be used for other error codes, not just the ones stored in the *ErrNo* variable. For example, the getsockopt() function can be used with the SO_ERROR argument to get the current error code. Unfortunately the codes returned are 10000 higher than the error codes usually found in *ErrNo*. For example getsockopt() returns a value of 10061 for 'connection refused' instead of 61. By subtracting 10000 from the returned value it is brought into the correct range so that SocketBaseTagList() will return the correct string.

```
if ( Error > 10000 ) Error -= 10000;
```

The above function will return a human readable string for *ErrNo* type codes. To convert the codes that are stored in the *HErrNo* variable the SocketBaseTagList() function can be used as well, but by using SBTC_HERRNOSTRPTR instead of SBTC_ERRNOSTRPTR.

The TCP-Connect example

This example uses a single non-blocking socket to create a connection to a server that accepts incoming TCP connections, which in this case is a web server. The example will make a connection and then send a simple GET request for the root page on the server. After that it will receive all the data that is being sent by the server and disconnect when everything has been received.

The example takes either the IP address or the hostname of the server to connect to as a command line argument and prints the results to the CLI/Shell window. Printing of the received data itself is commented out in the example as this floods the window with information, but can be enabled in the code to see what has been received.

Getting the address

The example takes a hostname or an IP address as its argument. The function gethostbyname() is used to resolve the hostname into an IP address. This function also accepts IP addresses as character strings and converts them into a binary IP address. When the name is successfully resolved the gethostbyname() function will return a hostent struct.

```
struct hostent * pHE = gethostbyname( pName );
if ( !pHE )
{
    // An error occurred, HErrNo should have more information
}

if ( pHE->h_length != 4 )
{
    return 0;
}

ULONG Addr = 0;
memcpy( (char *)&Addr, pHE->h_addr, sizeof( Addr ) );
```

The hostent struct is designed to support protocols other than the Internet protocols. To accommodate the addresses for these it returns the byte size of the address in the h_addr member. An IPv4 address is 32 bits, which is 4 bytes, and an answer of any other length can't be valid.

Preparing the socket

The *Type* argument of the socket() call decides which protocol is going to be used. For a UDP socket the type is SOCK_DGRAM, for a TCP socket the type needs to be SOCK_STREAM.

```
long Socket = socket( AF_INET, Type, 0 );
if ( Socket < 0 )
{
    // An error occurred, ErrNo should have more information
}
```

By default all sockets that are created use blocking mode. To change the socket to non-blocking mode the following call needs to be made. Enabling non-blocking mode on the socket will also enable asynchronous events on the socket.

```
ULONG Value = 1;
if ( IoctlSocket( Socket, FIONBIO, &Value ) < 0 )
{
    // An error occurred, ErrNo should have more information
}
```

In order to receive asynchronous events it is necessary to specify which events are of interest. Depending on the type of socket not all types of events will be used. For example the FD_ACCEPT and FD_CONNECT events are not used by SOCK_DGRAM type sockets while active TCP connections don't use the FD_ACCEPT event and passive TCP connections don't use the FD_CONNECT event.

```
ULONG Temp = FD_CONNECT | FD_READ | FD_WRITE | FD_CLOSE | FD_ERROR;
int Result = setsockopt( Socket, SOL_SOCKET, SO_EVENTMASK, &Temp, sizeof(Temp) );
if ( Result < 0 )
{
    // An error occurred, ErrNo should have more information
}
```

Connecting to the server

The connect() function expects a pointer to a sockaddr struct. There are different types of sockaddr struct, the version used for Internet connections is called sockaddr_in. It needs to be setup with the port number, which is 80 for standard HTTP web traffic, and it needs to be setup with the binary address that was obtained from gethostbyname() earlier.

```
struct sockaddr_in SockAddr;
SockAddr.sin_family = AF_INET;
SockAddr.sin_port = 80;
SockAddr.sin_addr.s_addr = Addr;

int Result = connect( Socket, (struct sockaddr *)&SockAddr, sizeof( SockAddr ) );
```

Due to the socket being non-blocking the function is very likely to return immediately with a value of -1. To find out if there indeed was an error the *ErrNo* variable needs to be checked.

```
if ( Result < 0 )
{
    if ( ErrNo != EINPROGRESS )
    {
        // An error has occurred, inform the user and stop the program.
    }
}
```

If the *ErrNo* value is EINPROGRESS then the creation of the connection has started but has not yet finished. If *ErrNo* has a different value then the connection process has not started and the value should indicate what the problem is. In this case the example will inform the user and close everything that was opened before exiting.

Asynchronous events

The result of the connection process will be communicated via the asynchronous events. These events are signalled to the example via the previously allocated Exec signal. The Exec Wait() function is used to put the program to sleep until such an event happens. To allow the user to interrupt the program by using the Ctrl+C user break signal the SIGBREAKF_CTRL_C mask is included as well.

```
ULONG Signals = Wait( SocketSignalMask | SIGBREAKF_CTRL_C );
```

The function will return a mask of the signal(s) that occurred during the wait, as multiple signals may have occurred at the same time. If the mask contains the SIGBREAKF_CTRL_C signal then the user issued a Ctrl+C break and the program can be terminated gracefully.

```
if ( Signals & SIGBREAKF_CTRL_C )
{
    // User break: terminate the program.
}
```

When the mask contains the bit set in the SocketSignalMask then there has been an asynchronous event. These events are processed by a separate function in the example and this function will return a negative value if there was an error or if the connection was closed. In those cases the program can be cleanly terminated as well. A return value of 0 means that the event was processed successfully and that the Exec Wait() function can be called again to await further signals.

```
if ( Signals & SocketSignalMask )
{
    if ( ProcessSocketSignal( RequestStr ) < 0 )
    {
        // Connection closed: terminate the program.
    }
}
```

In the ProcessSocketSignal() function the GetSocketEvents() function is called to get the descriptor of the socket for which the the event was generated as well as the mask of the event(s), as multiple events may have occurred since the last call to GetSocketEvents(). If the function returns -1 then there are no events.

```
ULONG EventMask=0;
int EventSocket = GetSocketEvents( &EventMask );
if ( EventSocket == -1 )
{
    // No events, not an error
    return 0;
}
```

Multiple events can and will happen at the same time. For example, when the connection process ends successfully on some network stacks both the FD_CONNECT and FD_WRITE event bits will be set in the EventMask variable. If there happens to be data waiting as well then the FD_READ may also be set. If the connection process ends with failure then both the FD_CONNECT and FD_ERROR bits could be set.

```
if ( EventMask & FD_CONNECT )
{
    // Successfully connected
```

The example uses the FD_CONNECT event to send the GET request string to the server. After sending the request string shutdown() is called with an argument value of 1 to indicate that no more data will be sent by the program.

```
int Len = strlen( pGetRequest );
int BytesDone = send( EventSocket, pGetRequest, Len, 0 );
if ( BytesDone < 0 )
{
    // There was an error sending.
}

shutdown( EventSocket, 1 );
}
```

When the server receives the GET request it will start sending data back. This can be a web page or an error message in HTML format. When the data is received by the network stack it is placed in its internal buffer and the FD_READ event is signalled to indicate that there is data to be read for the program. While the connection is active the network stack will continue to generate the FD_READ event while there still is data to be read from its internal buffers.

```
if ( EventMask & FD_READ )
{
    char Buffer[ 2048 ];
    int BytesDone = recv( EventSocket, Buffer, 2047, 0 );
    if ( BytesDone < 0 )
    {
        // There was an error reading the data.
    }
}
```

The recv() function reads only up to 2047 bytes into a 2048 buffer to keep space free to place a null-terminator, which is done for printing the received data to the console. In a non-trivial program adding this terminator is rarely required and the full buffer size can be used by recv().

When the server has finished sending its data it will shutdown the connection, which in turn will generate an FD_CLOSE event. This may happen before the example has read all data from the internal buffers of the network stack. All this data needs to be read from the internal buffers before CloseSocket() is called since this call will discard any unread data still in the internal buffers.

The example calls its ReadLastData() function before returning -1. Returning a negative number will end the main loop of the example and start the cleaning up before exiting gracefully.

```
if ( EventMask & FD_CLOSE )
{
    ReadLastData( EventSocket );
    return -1;
}
```

The ReadLastData() function will call the recv() function in a loop and exit the loop as soon as the recv() function no longer returns a positive value. When recv() returns a value of 0 then no more bytes are available in the internal buffer and the example can exit.

```
void ReadLastData( int Socket )
{
    char Buffer[ 2048 ];
    while ( 1 )
    {
        int BytesDone = recv( Socket, Buffer, 2047, 0 );
        if ( BytesDone == 0 )
        {
            // Last of the data has been read
            return;
        }

        if ( BytesDone < 0 )
        {
            // Error or EAGAIN
        }
        else
        {
            // Successful read of data
        }
    }
}
```

The example still tests for errors and EAGAIN although neither of these are likely to happen. The connection has already been closed by the server and the data that is being read is already present in the internal buffers.

Cleaning up

All that needs to be done before exiting is to call CloseSocket() with the socket descriptor as its argument and to call FreeSignal() with the bit number of the signal as its argument.

```
CloseSocket( Socket );
FreeSignal( SocketSignal );
```

Calling FreeSignal() is important for programs that are run from the CLI/Shell. These programs use the process space of the CLI/Shell and therefore also use the signals of the CLI/Shell. Not calling FreeSignal() will cause the CLI/Shell to run out of signals rather quickly. This is not an issue for programs that are run from the Workbench. These run in their own process, which get destroyed when the program exits.

The TCP-Server example

This example shows the other side of the TCP connection; the passive side. The example program will listen for incoming connections and accept them. It will then receive data and send a string back to the connecting host. To show an example of integrating Intuition messages the program will also open a simple window and when the close gadget of the window is clicked the program will gracefully exit. The program will also exit if the user issues a Ctrl+C break in the CLI/Shell.

For brevity only differences with the previous example will be highlighted, for example the creation of the socket is almost the same (the FD_ACCEPT event is selected instead of the FD_CONNECT event) and will therefore not be repeated here again.

Opening the window

A small window will be opened using the OpenWindowTagList() function. The window will have a title bar with a close gadget but no other gadgets. The only IDCMP class that is requested is the IDCMP_CLOSEWINDOW class.

```
static char  Title[] = "TCP Server";
ULONG WinTags[] = {
                        WA_Width,        200,
                        WA_Height,       100,
                        WA_Title,        (ULONG)&Title,
                        WA_IDCMP,        IDCMP_CLOSEWINDOW,
                        WA_Activate,     1,
                        WA_CloseGadget,  1
                  };

struct Window * pWin = OpenWindowTagList( NULL, (struct TagItem *)&WinTags );
```

The window communicates its IDCMP messages via a message port. This message port can be found via the UserPort member of the Window structure. Each message port uses an Exec signal to indicate that a new message is waiting. The bit number of the signal can be found in the mp_SigBit member of the message port structure.

The example converts this bit number into a mask so it can later be used with the Wait() function of the Exec library as part of the main processing loop.

```
ULONG WindowSigMask = 1 << pWin->UserPort->mp_SigBit;
```

Responding to incoming connections

A freshly created socket will have been assigned a random port number by the network stack. However, the client application connecting to this server expects the server to be on port 80. The socket of this server example therefore needs to be bound to port 80 before any connections can be accepted.

The bind() function expects a pointer to a sockaddr struct. Again the sockaddr_in version of the sockaddr structs is used. It needs to be setup with the port number, which is 80, and it needs to be setup with an address.

This address is used for systems with multiple network interfaces to bind the port to just one interface. It can also be used to bind the port only to the internal loopback interface (127.0.0.1) if the socket is only to be accessible by software running on the same computer. In this case it is fine to bind to all interfaces for which the pseudo address INADDR_ANY is used. This makes the port accessible for other hosts on the network as well as local software.

```
struct sockaddr_in SockAddr;
SockAddr.sin_family = AF_INET;
SockAddr.sin_port = 80;
SockAddr.sin_addr.s_addr = INADDR_ANY;

int Result = bind( Socket, (struct sockaddr *)&SockAddr, sizeof( SockAddr ) );
if ( Result < 0 )
{
    // An error occurred, ErrNo should have more information
}
```

If the call to bind() fails then this is usually because another TCP socket has already been bound to this port. In that case the *ErrNo* value will be EADDRINUSE and the matching error string will be "address already in use". There is no need to check *ErrNo* for EINPROGRESS since a call to bind() will never block, even on a blocking socket.

The socket is setup for incoming connections with a call to listen(), which takes the size of the waiting queue as an argument. Since this is a simple example that only processes one connection at a time there is no real need for a much larger queue than 1.

```
Result = listen( Socket, 1 );
if ( Result == -1 )
{
    // An error occurred, ErrNo should have more information
}
```

Asynchronous events

From this point everything that happens on the socket is triggered by asynchronous events. The Exec Wait() function is used again to put the program to sleep until one of the signals is activated. This time there are three signals now that the signal of the Window's IDCMP port has been added.

```
ULONG Signals = Wait( SocketSigMask | WindowSigMask | SIGBREAKF_CTRL_C );
```

When the Wait() call returns one or more signals may be active. The socket signal and the break signal are dealt with in a similar fashion as done in the previous example. When the signal of the window's IDCMP port is active the example's ProcessWindowMsg() function is called.

```
if ( Signals & WindowSigMask )
{
    Result = ProcessWindowMsg( pWin );
}
```

Although it is very unlikely for this trivial example, there could be more than one message on the Window's IDCMP port. When signalled the port should always be checked for messages until it indicates that there are no more messages. If the IDCMP_CLOSEWINDOW message is one of the messages on the port then the user clicked the window's close gadget. Returning a negative result from the ProcessWindowMsg() function gracefully exits the program.

```
int Result = 0;
struct Message * pMsg;
while ( pMsg = GetMsg( pWin->UserPort ) )
{
    struct IntuiMessage * pIMsg = (struct IntuiMessage *)pMsg;
    switch ( pIMsg->Class )
    {
        case IDCMP_CLOSEWINDOW :
            Result = -1;
            break;
    }

    ReplyMsg( pMsg );
}
```

When a client tries to connect to the port an asynchronous FD_ACCEPT event is signalled. To accept the connection the accept() function is called, which will return a new socket descriptor for this connection. Since this trivial example only accepts one connection at a time it will only accept a new connection while no others are in progress. It does this by checking the static NewSocket variable that will hold the socket descriptor of the current connection.

```
if ( EventMask & FD_ACCEPT )
{
    if ( NewSocket < 0 )
    {
        NewSocket = accept( EventSocket, NULL, 0 );
        if ( NewSocket == -1 )
        {
            // An error occurred, ErrNo should have more information
        }
        else
        {
            ULONG Tmp = FD_READ | FD_WRITE | FD_CLOSE | FD_ERROR;
            setsockopt( NewSocket, SOL_SOCKET, SO_EVENTMASK, &Tmp, sizeof(Tmp) );
        }
    }
}
```

If the main socket that was used to accept the connection is non-blocking then the new socket returned by accept() will also be non-blocking. By default the new socket will not have any events registered which is why the example immediately registers a number of events for the new socket.

When the FD_READ event is triggered the example will call recv() to get the data that was transmitted by the connected client. It will then call send() with the same buffer to return the data received from the client back to the client. Then it calls shutdown() with a value of 1 to indicate that no more data will be sent to the client.

```
if ( EventMask & FD_READ )
{
    char Buffer[ 1024 ];
    int BytesDone = recv( EventSocket, Buffer, 1023, 0 );
    if ( BytesDone > 0 )
    {
        int BytesSent = send( EventSocket, Buffer, BytesDone, 0 );
        if ( BytesSent < 0 )
        {
            // An error occurred, ErrNo should have more information
        }

        shutdown( EventSocket, 1 );
    }
}
```

When the remote client closes the connection an FD_CLOSE event is signalled. When this happens the socket of the new connection can be closed and the NewSocket variable set back to -1. The listening socket is not affected by this; new connections can still be accepted.

```
if ( EventMask & FD_CLOSE )
{
    if ( EventSocket == NewSocket )
    {
        CloseSocket( NewSocket );
        NewSocket = -1;
    }
}
```

Cleaning up

When exiting the program gracefully the window needs to be closed. Apart from the main listening socket it is also important to check if the connection socket is open and close that if it still is open. The reason for the connection socket to still be open can be the user clicking the window's close gadget while a connection is still in progress.

```
CloseWindow( pWin );
if ( NewSocket != -1 )
{
    CloseSocket( NewSocket );
}
CloseSocket( Socket );
FreeSignal( SocketSignal );
```

The UDP example

The executable created by this example can be used as a sender as well as a receiver. Its function is decided by the arguments used when it is run from the CLI/Shell. Without arguments it runs as a receiver on port 2080. When the first argument is a capital S it runs as a sender to port 2080 on the loopback interface. Other arguments can be added to change the port on the sender/receiver and to change the IP address for the sender. By opening two CLI/Shell windows the program can be used to send/receive UDP datagrams between the two instances. The program does not open any windows, but still accepts Ctrl+C as a break signal.

Once more only differences with the previous examples will be highlighted. The creation of the socket is almost the same although instead of a SOCK_STREAM type socket the type is now SOCK_DGRAM. The socket is still set to non-blocking mode and this time the FD_ACCEPT and FD_CONNECT events are not registered as they are not used by UDP sockets.

Sending the datagrams

In sender mode the program will send datagrams to the server and check for a reply and exit when a reply is received. If there is no reply then the program will exit after sending the 4th datagram. This can also be used to show the unreliable nature of UDP traffic; even when no receiver is present the sender will still successfully send the datagrams without getting any error messages.

To send the datagrams the sendto() function is used. This function requires a buffer with the data to send as well as a pointer to a sockaddr structure with the details of the destination. The example gets its destination as an IP address in a character string, which is converted into a 32 bits binary IP address with the inet_addr() function. This function does not resolve domain names or host names, only IP address in dotted notation are supported.

```
ULONG Addr = inet_addr( pAddress );
if ( Addr == INADDR_NONE )
{
    // The string did not contain a valid IP address.
}
```

The binary IP address is then inserted into the sockaddr_in structure together with the port number, similarly to how the TCP connect example did it.

```
struct sockaddr_in SockAddr;
SockAddr.sin_family = AF_INET;
SockAddr.sin_port = Port;
SockAddr.sin_addr.s_addr = Addr;
```

Each datagram can now be sent with a single call to sendto(). All that the buffer contains is a simple character string in this example. To create the interval between the sending of subsequent datagrams the Delay() function if the dos.library is used.

```
int BytesDone = sendto( Socket, pString, StringLen, 0,
                        (struct sockaddr*)&SockAddr, sizeof( SockAddr ) );
if ( BytesDone < 0 )
{
    // An error occurred, ErrNo should have more information
}
```

Receiving the datagrams

In receiver mode the example program will wait for datagrams and print a message each time one is received. The printed message will also show the IP address of the sender of the datagram. The program will also use the IP address and port of the sender to send a reply back to the sender, much in the same way as a DNS server would. The program will continue to wait for datagrams until the user issues a Ctrl+C break, which will gracefully exit the program.

Just like with the TCP server example the UDP socket needs to be bound to a port and an address with a call to bind(). If there is already a UDP socket bound to the port then the call to bind() will fail with an *ErrNo* value of EADDRINUSE and the error string will be "address already in use".

When a datagram is received the FD_READ event will be signalled. A call to recvfrom() then copies the received data into the supplied buffer and the address details of the sender are stored into the provided SockAddr structure.

```
char Buffer[ 1501 ];
struct sockaddr SockAddr;
long SockLen = sizeof( SockAddr );

int BytesDone = recvfrom( EventSocket, Buffer, 1500, 0, &SockAddr, &SockLen );
if ( BytesDone < 0 )
{
    // An error occurred, ErrNo should have more information
}
```

When recvfrom() returns the SockLen variable will contain the length of the structure returned in *SockAddr*. For an Internet address the structure returned will be a sockaddr_in structure and the *SockLen* variable should match this. Since the socket was opened as an Internet socket and the Amiga network stacks don't support other protocol families it is extremely unlikely that the returned structure is something else than a sockaddr_in structure.

To print the IP address the Inet_NtoA() function is used to convert the binary IP address into a human readable string. The port number of the sender is also printed and this shows how the randomly selected ephemeral port used by the sender changes with each run.

```
if ( SockLen == sizeof( struct sockaddr_in ) )
{
    struct sockaddr_in * RxAddr = (struct sockaddr_in *)&SockAddr;
    printf( "Received: %d bytes from: %s from port %lu\n", BytesDone,
                    Inet_NtoA( RxAddr->sin_addr.s_addr ), RxAddr->sin_port );
}
```

To send a reply back to the sender the same sockaddr_in structure and *SockLen* variable are used as arguments to the sendto() function. In the case of this example always the same string is sent back to the sender, regardless of what the received datagram actually contained.

```
const char Msg[] = "Message received!";
int BytesSent = sendto( EventSocket, Msg, strlen( Msg ), 0, &SockAddr, SockLen );
if ( BytesSent < 0 )
{
    // An error occurred, ErrNo should have more information
}
```

The UDP-Multicast example

The multicast example differs from the previous example in that it uses multicast addresses and that there is no reply message being sent by the receiver. The default multicast address used by the example is 228.0.0.1. The same default port (2080) is used as was used by the UDP example.

To send out multicast datagrams the sender does not need to do anything special - just send the datagrams to a multicast address. Since there will be no answer from any of the receivers the sender will just send 4 datagrams about a second apart and exit.

Joining the multicast group

The difference is greater at the receiver side since the receiver needs to join the multicast group before any datagrams sent to the multicast group will be received.

Joining is done by calling setsockopt() with the IP_ADD_MEMBERSHIP argument.

```
struct ip_mreq MultiReq;
MultiReq.imr_multiaddr.s_addr = inet_addr( pAddress );
MultiReq.imr_interface.s_addr = INADDR_ANY;

int Result = setsockopt( Socket, IPPROTO_IP, IP_ADD_MEMBERSHIP,
                            (const char *)&MultiReq, sizeof( MultiReq ) );
if ( Result < 0 )
{
    // An error occurred, ErrNo should have more information
}
```

Just like with bind() it is possible to limit the group to one interface, which is useful on hosts with multiple network interfaces. In this case any interface on the Amiga will be fine so the INADDR_ANY pseudo address is used again. This also includes the local loopback interface, which allows multicast data for this group but originating from the same host to be received.

There is no need to specify a port number since that has already been taken care of by the call to bind(). If the network stack does not support multicast then the result of the function call will be negative and *ErrNo* will be set to EADDRNOTAVAIL. The error string for this code is "Can't assign requested address". This can be the case with older network stacks that do not implement multicasting. Since these stacks can still be in use it is important for programs to catch this error and give the user a suitable error message.

Leaving the multicast group

When the program is done receiving it should leave the multicast group. That is also done by calling setsockopt(), but this time with the IP_DROP_MEMBERSHIP argument. It uses the same struct ip_mreq for this call as it used to join the group.

```
int Result = setsockopt( Socket, IPPROTO_IP, IP_DROP_MEMBERSHIP,
                            (const char *)&MultiReq, sizeof( MultiReq ) );
if ( Result < 0 )
{
    // An error occurred, ErrNo should have more information
}
```

When a program is using recvfrom() to receive multicast datagrams then the address details of the sender are placed into the sockaddr_in structure just like with the UDP example. The IP address in the sockaddr_in will be the actual IP address of the sender, not the multicast address of the group. This address can be used for contacting the sender directly, outside of the multicast group.

6. Sockets in assembler

The bsdsocket.library can also be accessed by software written in assembly. Since the assembly code will be calling the same functions as the C code there will be a lot of similarities between the two. However, the documentation and header files of the bsdsocket.library are geared towards C programming. This makes it a little more work for the assembler programmer to use the library, and it means that it is sometimes necessary to read the C header files to extract some of the information needed, like the value of some of the constants.

The 'lvo' directory in the examples archive contains a number of assembly header files. These header files contain the Library Vector Offset, or LVO, for each of the functions in the library. Of these, the bsdsocket_lib.i file is the one that contains the vector offsets for the functions of the bsdsocket.library.

For brevity the code shown here has most of the error recovery removed, the full source in the download will have most of this implemented. There will be small differences between the code here in the book and the code in the download; this is again mainly done for brevity.

All these examples are meant to be run from the CLI/Shell and not from the Workbench. This allows the examples to use the CLI/Shell window to output status.

Setting up

The bsdsocket.library needs to be opened and closed exactly like this is done for any other library on the system. Since it is quite possible that the library is not available any non-trivial program should show a suitable error message when the library happens to be missing.

Increasing the stack size

The default stack size used by AmigaOS is not large enough for some of the functions provided by the bsdsocket.library. This can lead to the program overrunning the stack, which may cause odd crashes and system reboots.

The amount of stack required by a program can be specified via the 'stack cookie', which is a string embedded in the program that informs the OS of the amount of stack required. The following cookie requests a stack of 10240 bytes.

```
StackCookie:    DC.B    "$STACK:10240",0
```

Writing to to the console

The example code prints messages to the CLI/Shell console to show its progress. When the program starts it calls the Output() function of the dos.library to get the file handle needed to write to the console. This is a standard DOS file handle that can be used to write to the console in the same way as writing to a file.

```
MOVE.L   DosBase(PC),a6        ; a6 = DOS
JSR      _LVOOutput(a6)
MOVE.L   d0,OutHand            ; BPTR console handle
```

The print function expects a pointer to a null-terminated character string in A0. It then counts the length of the string, excluding the null-terminator, and calls the dos.library Write() function to write the string to the output handle.

```
Print:       MOVEM.L d0-d7/a0-a6,-(a7)   ; Preserve all registers
             MOVE.L  OutHand(PC),d1      ; BPTR console handle
             MOVE.L  a0,d2               ; APTR String to print

             MOVEQ.L #0,d3               ; Reset counter in D3
.CountLoop   TST.B   (a0)+               ; Check for null-terminator
             BEQ.B   .Counted            ; Found it? Done counting
             ADDQ.L  #1,d3               ; Another char counted
             BRA.B   .CountLoop          ; Keep counting

.Counted     MOVE.L  DosBase(PC),a6      ; A6 = DOS
             JSR     _LVOWrite(a6)       ; Print string to console
             MOVEM.L (a7)+,d0-d7/a0-a6   ; Restore original register values
             RTS
```

To ensure that the function can be called from anywhere it preserves all registers on the stack and retrieves them before returning. While the Write() function is unlikely to use all the registers, for this example simply storing all registers makes the intent more obvious.

Sometimes the string printed needs additional information to be inserted. For example the string 'Received 240 bytes' has the number 240 inserted. In C this is done with the printf() function. The Exec library's RawDoFmt() function provides some of the functionality of sprintf() and is used by the example's Printf() function to achieve a similar goal. It expects the format string pointer in A0 and a pointer to the data stream in A1. This data stream is nothing else than an array of DWORDs, one for each element that needs to be inserted into the string.

```
MOVE.L   4.w,a6              ; a6 = Exec Base
LEA.L    PutChar(PC),a2      ; APTR Callback function
LEA.L    Buffer,a3           ; APTR Buffer to print resulting string to
JSR      _LVORawDoFmt(a6)
```

The RawDoFmt() function expects a pointer to a callback function in A2. This function will get the character to store in D0 and the pointer to the location to store it to in A3.

```
PutChar:        MOVE.B  d0,(a3)+                        ; Place char into string
                RTS
```

The RawDoFmt() function itself will not touch A3 between subsequent calls to the callback. This allows the callback function to update A3 as required.

Signals and error codes

An Exec signal needs to be allocated so that the socket library can use it for signalling asynchronous events. The Exec function AllocSignal() is used to allocate a free signal. It will return the bit number of the signal when successful. This bit number then needs to be converted to a bitmask for the SocketBaseTagList() function and later the Exec Wait() function.

```
        MOVE.L   4.W,a6                  ; a6 = ExecBase
        MOVEQ.L  #-1,d0                  ; Any free signal
        JSR      _LVOAllocSignal(a6)
        MOVE.L   d0,Signal               ; Store the signal number
        BMI.W    .NoSignal               ; Negative? No free signals

        MOVEQ.L  #1,d1                   ; Set bit 0 in D1
        ASL.L    d0,d1                   ; Shift it left "signal number" times
        MOVE.L   d1,SignalMask           ; Store the signal mask
```

The newly created signal mask is communicated to the bsdsocket.library with a call to the SocketBaseTagList() function.

The socket interface uses two variables to store error codes in, *errno* and *h_errno*. The bsdsocket.library needs a pointer to these variables in order to be able to access them. This can be done via the same call to SocketBaseTagList() as is used to set the signal mask.

```
        MOVE.L   SockBase(PC),a6         ; a6 = SockBase
        LEA.L    .Tags(PC),a0            ; APTR tags
        JSR      _LVOSocketBaseTagList(a6)

.Tags           DC.L    SBTM_SETVAL|SBTC_SIGEVENTMASK
SignalMask:     DC.L    0
                DC.L    SBTM_SETVAL|SBTC_ERRNOLONGPTR
                DC.L    ErrNo
                DC.L    SBTM_SETVAL|SBTC_HERRNOLONGPTR
                DC.L    HErrNo
                DC.L    TAG_END
```

Getting error code information

When the socket functions indicate that an error has occurred the code that describes the error can be found in the *ErrNo* variable (or the *HErrNo* variable for a small number of functions). The socket library provides a method to convert the *ErrNo* code into a human readable string by calling SocketBaseTagList() with SBTM_GETVAL | SBTC_ERRNOSTRPTR as the tag. The data for the tag is the error code.

When the SocketBaseTagList() function returns the error code in the tag data will have been replaced with a pointer to the human readable error string.

```
                MOVE.L   ErrNo(PC),d0                ; LONG error code
                CMPI.L   #10000,d0                   ; Code in the 10000 range?
                BMI.B    .CodeOK                     ; No. No need to change
                SUBI.L   #10000,d0                   ; Change to normal range

.CodeOK         LEA.L    .Tags(PC),a0                ; APTR tags
                MOVE.L   d0,4(a0)                    ; Place error code in taglist
                JSR      _LVOSocketBaseTagList(a6)
                TST.L    d0                          ; Success?
                BNE.B    .TagErr                     ; No! Do not print

.Tags           DC.L     SBTM_GETVAL|SBTC_ERRNOSTRPTR
                DC.L     0
                DC.L     TAG_END
```

When the getsockopt() function is used with the SO_ERROR argument to get the current error code then it will return error codes that are 10000 higher than the error codes usually found in *ErrNo*. For example a value of 10061 for 'connection refused' instead of 61. By subtracting 10000 from the *ErrNo* the value is brought into the correct range to get the matching string.

The TCP-Connect example

This example uses a single non-blocking socket to create a connection to a server that accepts incoming TCP connections on port 80, which is the default port used by web servers. After creating the connection, the example will send a simple 'GET request' to the server to request the root web page. After that it will receive all the data that is being sent by the server and exit when everything has been received.

The example takes either the IP address or the hostname of the server to connect to as a command line argument. It can be interrupted at any time by issuing a Ctrl+C break in the console.

Getting the address

The example takes a hostname or an IP address as a command line argument. The function gethostbyname() is used to resolve the hostname into a binary IP address. This function also accepts IP addresses as character strings and converts them into a binary IP address also. When the name is successfully resolved the gethostbyname() function will return a pointer to a hostent struct.

```
MOVE.L   SockBase(PC),a6          ; a6 = SockBase
LEA.L    HostName,a0              ; APTR Hostname string
JSR      _LVOgethostbyname(a6)
TST.L    d0                       ; Successful result?
BEQ.B    .NoAddr                  ; No? Show error message

MOVEA.L  d0,a0                    ; APTR Hostent struct
CMPI.L   #4,h_length(a0)          ; LONG Length: must be 4
BNE.B    .NoAddr                  ; No? Not an IPv4 address!

MOVEA.L  h_addr_list(a0),a0       ; APTR 1st addr in list
MOVEA.L  (a0),a0                  ; APTR IP address
MOVE.L   (a0),d0                  ; DWORD IP address
RTS
```

The h_length field is checked to see if the result has 4 bytes. If not, then the result is not an IPv4 address. That is an unlikely situation at the moment as the Amiga network stacks only support IPv4. In the future these may be extended to support more protocols like IPv6. At that point the gethostbyname() function may actually return an IPv6 address.

The returned hostent struct contains a pointer to a list of addresses. This list is basically nothing but an array of pointers with the last one a NULL. To get the first address in the list the example gets the pointer to the list from h_addr_list and uses this to get the first pointer in the list. This pointer points to a DWORD which holds the 32 bits binary IPv4 address.

Preparing the socket

The *type* argument of the socket() call decides which protocol is going to be used. For a UDP socket the type should be SOCK_DGRAM, for a TCP socket the type needs to be set to SOCK_STREAM. In both cases the *domain* argument is set to AF_INET and the *protocol* argument is set to zero.

```
MOVE.L   SockBase(PC),a6          ; a6 = SockBase
MOVEQ.L  #AF_INET,d0              ; LONG domain
MOVEQ.L  #SOCK_STREAM,d1          ; LONG type
MOVEQ.L  #0,d2                    ; LONG protocol
JSR      _LVOsocket(a6)
MOVE.L   d0,Socket                ; Store socket descriptor
BMI.B    .NoSocket                ; Negative result?
```

In order to receive asynchronous events it is necessary to specify the events that are of interest. Depending on the type of socket not all types of events will be required. For example the FD_ACCEPT and FD_CONNECT events are not used by SOCK_DGRAM type sockets while active TCP connections don't use the FD_ACCEPT event and passive TCP connections don't use FD_CONNECT.

The events are selected by creating a mask with all the events of interest. Then the setsockopt() function is called with the SO_EVENTMASK option and a pointer to the mask in A0. Since the mask is a DWORD the *optlen* argument is set to 4.

```
           MOVE.L   SockBase(PC),a6        ; a6 = SockBase
           MOVE.L   Socket(PC),d0          ; LONG sd
           MOVE.L   #SOL_SOCKET,d1         ; LONG level
           MOVE.L   #SO_EVENTMASK,d2       ; LONG optname
           MOVEQ.L  #4,d3                  ; LONG optlen
           LEA.L    .EventMask(PC),a0      ; APTR optval
           JSR      _LVOsetsockopt(a6)

.EventMask  DC.L     FD_CONNECT|FD_READ|FD_WRITE|FD_CLOSE|FD_ERROR
```

By default all sockets are created as blocking sockets. To change the socket to non-blocking mode the following call to IoctlSocket() needs to be made.

```
           MOVE.L   SockBase(PC),a6        ; a6 = SockBase
           MOVE.L   Socket(PC),d0          ; LONG sd
           MOVE.L   #FIONBIO,d1            ; LONG request
           LEA.L    .Arg(PC),a0            ; APTR argp
           JSR      _LVOIoctlSocket(a6)

.Arg        DC.L     1
```

Please note that enabling non-blocking mode on the socket will also enable asynchronous events to be signalled on the socket.

Connecting to the server

The connect() function expects a pointer to a sockaddr_in structure. This is the version of the sockaddr structure used for IPv4 connections. The structure is laid out in memory and has been pre-filled with the address family and port number. The binary IPv4 address that was obtained from gethostbyname() previously needs to be copied into the field with the *.IPAddress* label.

```
.SockAddrIn   DC.W    AF_INET      ; Family
              DC.W    80           ; Port number
.IPAddress    DC.L    0            ; IP address
              DCB.B   8,0          ; sin_zero
```

The connect() function is then called and its return value is checked. Since the socket is non-blocking the result is most likely to be negative, with a value of EINPROGRESS in *ErrNo*. This means that the connection process is on-going. If a different value is found in *ErrNo* then an error has occurred and the connection process will not have been started.

```
MOVE.L    SockBase(PC),a6        ; a6 = SockBase
MOVE.L    Socket(PC),d0          ; LONG sd
MOVEQ.L   #16,d1                 ; LONG addrlen
LEA.L     .SockAddrIn(PC),a0     ; APTR addr
JSR       _LVOconnect(a6)
TST.L     d0                     ; Check the result
BEQ.B     .NoErr                 ; Zero = no error
CMPI.L    #EINPROGRESS,ErrNo     ; Just an "in progress"?
BNE.B     .Close                 ; No - a real error
```

Asynchronous events

The result of the connection process will be communicated via the asynchronous events. These events are signalled via the previously allocated Exec signal. The Exec Wait() function is used to put the program to sleep until a signal is activated. To allow the user to interrupt the program with Ctrl+C the SIGBREAKF_CTRL_C signal is included as well.

```
.MainLoop    MOVE.L    4.W,a6                       ; a6 = ExecBase
             MOVE.L    SignalMask(PC),d0            ; ULONG Socket signal
             ORI.L     #SIGBREAKF_CTRL_C,d0         ; ULONG Ctrl+C break signal
             JSR       _LVOWait(a6)                 ; Wait for signals
```

The Wait() function will use D0 to return a mask of the signal(s) that occurred. It is possible that more than one signal bit in the returned bit mask is set. If the SIGBREAKF_CTRL_C bit is set in the returned mask then the user issued a Ctrl+C break and the program can be exited gracefully.

```
MOVE.L    d0,d1
ANDI.L    #SIGBREAKF_CTRL_C,d0     ; User Ctrl+C break?
BNE.B     .UserBreak              ; Yes.
```

When the returned mask contains the *SignalMask* bit then there has been an asynchronous socket event. These are processed by a separate function in the example and that function will return a non-zero value if there was an error or if the connection was closed. In those cases the program can exit, otherwise the Exec Wait() function will be called again to await further events.

```
AND.L    SignalMask(PC),d1        ; Socket signal?
BEQ.B    .MainLoop                ; No. Wait again.
BSR.W    ProcessSocket            ; Yes. Process socket event
BNE.B    .Close                   ; Non-zero = error or connection gone
BRA.B    .MainLoop                ; Keep looping
```

In the example's ProcessSocket() function the GetSocketEvents() function is called, which will return the descriptor of the socket as well as the mask of the event(s) that occurred. If there are no events then the function will return -1. The example then stores the socket descriptor in register D7 so that it can be used later by the various socket functions.

```
ProcessSocket: MOVE.L  SockBase(PC),a6          ; A6 = SockBase
               LEA.L   .Events(PC),a0           ; APTR events_ptr
               JSR     _LVOGetSocketEvents(a6)
               MOVE.L  d0,d7                    ; Event socket descriptor
               BMI.B   .Done                    ; No socket! Nothing to do
```

Multiple events can happen at the same time. For example, when the connection process ends successfully on some networks stacks both the FD_CONNECT and FD_WRITE event bits will be set in the EventMask variable. When the connection process ends with failure then both the FD_CONNECT and FD_ERROR bits could be set. Checking for an event is therefore done using a bitwise AND with the event mask.

```
               MOVE.L  .Events(PC),d0           ; Get the mask of events
               ANDI.W  #FD_CONNECT,d0           ; Is the FD_CONNECT bit set?
               BEQ.B   .NotConn                 ; No. Not a connect event
               BSR.B   EventConnect             ; Yes. Process the event
```

The functions that each process a particular event are all called as subroutines. This makes it simple to ensure that upon returning from these function the next events will be checked.

When the connection is established the FD_CONNECT event will be signalled. This in turn will cause the EventConnect() function to be called. This function will print that the FD_CONNECT event has occurred and then send the GET request to the server. The request string was prepared earlier and placed in the *Buffer* area. Before the string can be sent the EventConnect() function needs to count the length of the string.

```
               LEA.L   Buffer,a0                ; APTR Get request
               MOVEA.L a0,a1                    ; Make copy for counting

               MOVEQ.L #0,d1                    ; Length counter
.Count         TST.B   (a1)+                    ; Null-terminator?
               BEQ.B   .Done                    ; Yes. Done counting
               ADDQ.L  #1,d1                    ; Count another char
               BRA.B   .Count                   ; Do until terminator

.Done          MOVE.L  d7,d0                    ; LONG socket descriptor
               MOVEQ.L #0,d2                    ; LONG flags
               MOVE.L  SockBase(PC),a6          ; a6 = SockBase
               JSR     _LVOsend(a6)
               MOVE.L  d0,.FmtData              ; Copy result for printing
```

The send() function will return the number of bytes sent, or a negative value in case of an error. For simplicity the example ignores the possibility of an error at this stage since errors will be highly unlikely and also should in theory be picked up by the FD_ERROR event. For a non-trivial program it is recommended to always check all return values of the socket functions to ensure that errors will be detected early and that the program is not going to wait for asynchronous events that may now never happen.

The GET request string is all that the example will be sending to the server. To indicate that no more data will be sent the example calls the shutdown() function with an argument value of 1. The server now knows that it can terminate the connection as soon as it has dealt with the request.

```
MOVE.L   d7,d0                    ; LONG socket descriptor
MOVEQ.L  #1,d1                    ; LONG how = no more sending
MOVE.L   SockBase(PC),a6          ; a6 = SockBase
JSR      _LVOshutdown(a6)
```

The server will in response to the request send out data. This could be the root document the request asked for, but could also be a 'document not found' error message or a 'document has moved' message. In all of these cases the message returned will be formatted as a text document in HTML format.

Receiving the server's response will result in an FD_READ event being signalled. This event will cause the example's EventRead() routine to be called, which will call recv() to copy the incoming data into the buffer.

```
MOVE.L   SockBase(PC),a6          ; a6 = SockBase
MOVE.L   d7,d0                    ; LONG socket descriptor
MOVE.L   #4095,d1                 ; LONG buffer length
MOVEQ.L  #0,d2                    ; LONG flags
LEA.L    Buffer,a0                ; APTR buffer
JSR      _LVOrecv(a6)
MOVE.L   d0,.FmtData              ; Copy result for printing
BMI.B    PrintErr                 ; Negative? That's an error.
```

The recv() function reads only up to 4095 bytes into a 4096 buffer to keep space free to place a null-terminator, which is done to allow for printing the received data to the console. In a non-trivial program adding this terminator is rarely required and the full buffer size can be used by recv().

If the server sends more than 4095 bytes then the rest of the data will still be kept in the internal buffer of the networking stack. While the connection is still open this will cause the FD_READ event to be signalled again until there is no more data to be read from the internal buffer. While the program is still reading from the internal buffer the server may have sent all its data and close the connection. This will cause the FD_CLOSE event to be signalled, even though there may be much more data to be retrieved from the internal buffers. On some network stacks this will also stop any more FD_READ events from being signalled.

Closing the socket at this point will discard any unread data that may still be in the internal buffers. Before closing the socket all data needs to be read from the internal buffers. The example does this as part of the EventClose() function, which first prints a short message to the CLI/Shell window and will then call recv() until no more data is present (or until an error occurs).

```
.Loop        MOVE.L   d7,d0              ; LONG socket descriptor
             MOVE.L   #4095,d1           ; LONG buffer length
             MOVEQ.L  #0,d2              ; LONG flags
             LEA.L    Buffer,a0          ; APTR buffer
             JSR      _LVOrecv(a6)
             MOVE.L   d0,.FmtData        ; Copy result for printing
             BMI.B    PrintErr           ; Negative? That's an error.
             BEQ.B    .NoData            ; Zero means no more data

             LEA.L    .FmtStr(PC),a0     ; APTR FormatString
             LEA.L    .FmtData(PC),a1    ; APTR Data for the string
             BSR.W    Printf
             BRA.B    .Loop              ; Read more data
```

When the number of bytes to be read from the internal buffers reaches zero the EventClose() function returns to the ProcessSocket() function. The ProcessSocket() function will then return with a negative value in D0. This negative value indicates to the main loop that the program can now gracefully exit.

Closing and cleaning up

When all the data has been received the socket can be closed safely.

```
             MOVE.L   SockBase(PC),a6    ; a6 = SockBase
             MOVE.L   Socket(PC),d0      ; Socket descriptor
             JSR      _LVOCloseSocket(a6)
```

Then the Exec signal can be freed. Freeing the signal is necessary since it is owned by the CLI/Shell process and if it is not freed each time then the CLI/Shell process will run out of its 16 signals. The last step is closing the bsdsocket.library. This can be done the usual way.

```
             MOVE.L   4.W,a6             ; a6 = ExecBase
             MOVE.L   Signal(PC),d0      ; Signal number
             JSR      _LVOFreeSignal(a6)

             MOVE.L   SockBase(PC),a1
             JSR      _LVOCloseLibrary(a6)
```

The TCP-Server example

This example shows the other side of the TCP connection; the passive side. The example program will use a non-blocking socket to listen for incoming connections and accept them. It will then receive the data sent by the connecting host and after that send a character string back to that host. The program will exit when the user issues a Ctrl+C break in the CLI/Shell.

For brevity only differences with the previous example will be highlighted, for example the creation of the socket is almost the same (the FD_ACCEPT event is requested instead of the FD_CONNECT event) and will therefore not be repeated here again.

The example takes no arguments from the command line.

Preparing for incoming connections

After creating the socket, enabling the non-blocking mode and selecting the asynchronous events that are required the socket can be setup for incoming connections. First the socket needs to be bound to port 80, the default port used by web servers.

This is done via a call to bind(), which requires the socket descriptor as well as a pointer to the sockaddr_in structure and its length as arguments.

```
        MOVE.L    Socket(PC),d0          ; LONG sd
        MOVEQ.L   #16,d1                 ; LONG addrlen
        LEA.L     .SockAddrIn(PC),a0     ; APTR addr
        JSR       _LVObind(a6)
        TST.L     d0                     ; Check the result
        BEQ.B     .Listen                ; Zero = no error
```

In this case the sockaddr_in structure is already filled in. The address of INADDR_ANY is used to bind the socket to all local interfaces. This allows the socket to accept connections from the machine itself (via the loopback interface) as well as the wider network.

```
.SockAddrIn     DC.W      AF_INET        ; Family
                DC.W      80             ; Port number
                DC.L      INADDR_ANY     ; IP address
                DCB.B     8,0            ; sin_zero
```

After the socket has been bound to port 80 it is set in "listen" mode. The example will only accept one connection at a time so a backlog of only 1 will be sufficient.

```
        MOVE.L    Socket(PC),d0          ; LONG sd
        MOVEQ.L   #1,d1                  ; LONG backlog
        JSR       _LVOlisten(a6)
        TST.L     d0                     ; Check the result
        BEQ.B     .MainLoop              ; Zero = no error
```

Accepting an incoming connection

An incoming connection from a client is signalled with the FD_ACCEPT asynchronous event. When the example gets that event it calls the accept() function to accept the incoming connection. The call to accept() will return a new socket descriptor in D0. It will also fill in the sockaddr_in structure with the address details of the remote host.

```
MOVE.L   d7,d0                        ; LONG sd
LEA.L    .SockAddrIn(PC),a0           ; APTR addr
LEA.L    .SockAddrLen(PC),a1          ; APTR addrlen
JSR      _LVOaccept(a6)
TST.L    d0                           ; Check the result
BMI.W    PrintErr                     ; Negative? That is an error
```

The new socket descriptor will be stored in the *NewSocket* location. A value of -1 in this location means that there currently is no connection. Since this example only handles one connection at a time the value in this location is checked and if there is already an ongoing connection then the new socket that accept() returned is immediately closed.

```
TST.L    NewSocket                    ; Already connected?
BMI.B    .NewConn                     ; No. Use this one
JSR      _LVOCloseSocket(a6)          ; Yes. Close the new socket
```

The new socket will be non-blocking, just like the listening socket. But it will not yet have any asynchronous events selected. The example therefore needs to select the events it requires. The new socket is already connected and will not need the FD_CONNECT or FD_ACCEPT events.

```
.NewConn        MOVE.L   d0,NewSocket           ; Store the new socket
                MOVE.L   #SOL_SOCKET,d1         ; LONG level
                MOVE.L   #SO_EVENTMASK,d2       ; LONG optname
                MOVEQ.L  #4,d3                  ; LONG optlen
                LEA.L    .EventMask(PC),a0      ; APTR optval
                JSR      _LVOsetsockopt(a6)

.EventMask      DC.L     FD_READ|FD_WRITE|FD_CLOSE|FD_ERROR
```

The accept() function filled a sockaddr_in structure with the IP address and port number of the client that made the incoming connection. Before this information is printed to the CLI/Shell window the IP address (in binary format) is converted by the Inet_NtoA() function into a string.

```
LEA.L    .SockAddrIn(PC),a0           ; APTR sockaddr_in
MOVE.L   sin_addr(a0),d0              ; LONG client IP address
JSR      _LVOInet_NtoA(a6)
```

The Inet_NtoA() function returns a pointer to the string in register D0. This pointer is then placed into the data stream of a format string, which is then printed to the console.

Transferring data

The example will not immediately transmit any data, but wait for the connecting host to transmit something first. As soon as the host sends data the FD_READ event will be signalled. The example will then read the data that was sent.

```
MOVE.L    d7,d0              ; LONG socket descriptor
MOVE.L    #4095,d1           ; LONG buffer length
MOVEQ.L   #0,d2              ; LONG flags
LEA.L     Buffer,a0          ; APTR buffer
JSR       _LVOrecv(a6)
MOVE.L    d0,.RdFmtData      ; Copy result for printing
BMI.B     .Negative          ; Negative? Maybe an error
```

With a non-blocking socket a negative return in D0 from recv() may not actually be an error. It could mean that there is no data to read yet, which is indicated with a value of EAGAIN in *ErrNo*.

If there is a positive return value from recv() then that indicates the number of bytes received. The example does not use the data that was received and simply sends the same hardcoded string back to any client that connects.

```
MOVE.L    d7,d0                  ; LONG socket descriptor
MOVEQ.L   #WriteDataLen,d1       ; LONG buffer length
MOVEQ.L   #0,d2                  ; LONG flags
LEA.L     WriteData(PC),a0       ; APTR Data to send
JSR       _LVOsend(a6)
MOVE.L    d0,.WrFmtData          ; Copy result for printing
```

```
WriteData       DC.B    "The data to be sent back to the connecting client",10
WriteDataLen = *-WriteData
```

This is all the data that the example is going to send. To signal this to the connecting host a call to shutdown() is made with a *how* argument of 1.

```
MOVE.L    d7,d0              ; LONG socket descriptor
MOVEQ.L   #1,d1              ; LONG how = no more sending
JSR       _LVOshutdown(a6)
```

Closing the connection

When both sides of the connection have issued a call to shutdown() the connection can be closed. This is signalled by the FD_CLOSE event. The example uses this event to close the socket.

```
MOVE.L    d7,d0                  ; LONG socket descriptor
JSR       _LVOCloseSocket(a6)
MOVE.L    NewSocket(PC),d0       ; LONG sd of client connection
CMP.L     d0,d7                  ; Is it the client socket?
BNE.B     .Done                  ; No? Odd that!
MOVE.L    #-1,NewSocket          ; Yes. Clear socket descriptor.
```

The socket descriptor of the event is compared with the one stored in the *NewSocket* location. In this case it is highly unlikely that this will be a different socket descriptor. When the event socket is indeed the connection socket then the *NewSocket* location will get a value of -1 to allow another connection to be accepted. Closing the connection socket will not affect the listening socket, which will still be open and listening for incoming connections.

Cleaning up

The only way to stop the example is by issuing a user break (Ctrl+C) in the CLI/Shell window. The user break will be signalled via the SIGBREAKF_CTRL_C signal. The example uses this to do a clean exit. The listening socket can be closed immediately. It will never be used for a connection and calling shutdown() on it is not needed.

```
.Close          MOVE.L  SockBase(PC),a6       ; a6 = SockBase
                MOVE.L  Socket(PC),d0         ; LONG socket descriptor
                JSR     _LVOCloseSocket(a6)
```

The value of the *NewSocket* location is also checked and if it is not negative then that means that there is still a connection open on it. Since the example is exiting there is no need to shut it down gracefully and the socket is closed without calling shutdown(). This will simply reset the connection and inform the connected host that the connection has been closed.

```
                MOVE.L  NewSocket(PC),d0      ; LONG socket descriptor
                BMI.B   .Exit                 ; Negative = already closed
                JSR     _LVOCloseSocket(a6)
```

7. Secure networking

The IP protocols transport the data as-is. When a browser downloads a web page over HTTP it will use a standard TCP connection. The request the browser sent will be in text format and server will use as many segments as required to transport the web page data to the browser. All routers along the way can see the content of all the segments, regardless if the segments contain publicly available information or highly private information like banking details.

This gets even worse on wireless networks where anybody connected to the network (like in a coffee shop or cafe) can potentially see all packets sent and received by the other users of the network. When using standard IP connectivity without encryption anybody on the wireless network can see what is in the packets.

When the Internet grew from being a network of universities and other places of research into a public network accessible by anybody the need for secure connections became more and more clear. At first the SSL (Secure Socket Layer) standard was proposed and implemented, but by version 3.0 changes had to be made to make it more secure. Since these changes were not backwards compatible with SSL a name change was proposed. The new standard was then renamed to TLS (Transport Layer Security) of which the first version was TLS 1.0. The current version (at the time of writing) is TLS 1.3. The term SSL is still used a lot, even when TLS is actually being used, for example the libraries are still called OpenSSL and AmiSSL and most function names are prefixed with SSL_.

This chapter will take a look at the way the security protocols work in order to provide some background information. The first section will explain some of the algorithms used and the second section will look more closely at how these algorithms are used with SSL/TLS.

Algorithms

There are different types of algorithm that are designed to be used for different purposes. This section will explain more about these different types of algorithm and how these are used.

The TLS standard does not depend on one single algorithm per type, it uses a collection of algorithms so that when new algorithms are developed they can be added and older ones can be removed. This can be done without necessarily needing to change the standard or make existing applications incompatible with newer ones. When two systems connect with each other they perform a handshake and during that handshake they will select the best algorithms to use from the list of algorithms that both sides support.

Hashes

A cryptographic hash is a large number created by a hashing algorithm that takes an amount of data as its input. A hash is usually more than 128 bits in size, for example the SHA-256 algorithm creates a hash of 256 bits. More bits means more security but also requires more calculations. A cryptographic hashing algorithm is designed in such a way that a small change in the input data will result in a large change in the hash that is created.

When different inputs generate the same hash then this is called a 'collision'.Collisions will always be part of a hashing algorithm since all it does in principle is reduce a block of data that could be many mega bytes in size into a number of a much smaller number of bytes. However, for a good cryptographic hashing algorithm it is important that it is not possible to manipulate the input data in such a way that it produces a specific hash as its output.

What this means is that when a good cryptographic hashing algorithm is used to create a hash of a file then any changes to the file will result in a different hash. At the same time it must not be possible to make more changes to the file in order to make it match the original hash again. This makes the hash a very reliable method for detecting that file has been modified.

Ciphers

An algorithm used to encrypt and decrypt data is called a cipher. Ciphers use keys to encrypt and decrypt the data and the more bits the key is long, the more secure the data is. With a key that is too short it would be possible to decrypt the data by trying all possible keys until the correct one is found – this process is called 'brute forcing'.

Take for example a very short key that is 32 bits long and an algorithm that takes 1 hour to try all possible combinations. With each bit added to the key the time it takes to try all combinations will double. For a 128 bits key this same algorithm will take 2^{96} hours to try all combinations, which is such a large number that it is likely that the sun will have gone out long before the correct key will have been found.

Even with a long key encrypted data could be cracked if a mathematical shortcut is found to the decryption, or if a particular pattern is found in the output that gives insight in the value of the key itself. This is one of the reasons why the TLS algorithm is not build on a particular cipher; so that ciphers that have been proved to have flaws can easily be removed from use.

There are two distinctive types of cipher; the symmetric cipher and the asymmetric cipher. Both types are used for TLS encrypted connections.

Symmetric ciphers

Symmetric ciphers use the same key for encryption and decryption. The downside of using the same key for encryption and decryption is that both parties need to have the same key in their possession and they both need to keep it a secret.

In the image below Alice wants to encrypt a document before sending it to Bob so that Eve can't intercept it or tamper with it. Alice has created a key for the symmetric cipher and uses that key to encrypt the document. Bob receives the encrypted document but will also need Alice's key to decrypt it. Alice now needs to find a secure way to communicate the key to Bob so that Eve will not be able to intercept the key and then decrypt the message. Sending the key using the same communication method as the encrypted document is therefore not a secure option.

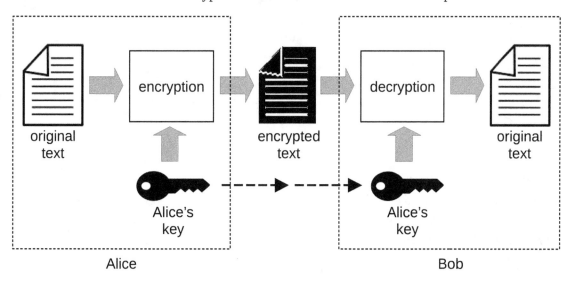

Asymmetric ciphers

Asymmetric ciphers have two separate keys; one of these keys is kept private, while the other one can be made public. While the two keys are related it is not possible to create the private key from the public key.

An asymmetric cipher allows anybody to encrypt data using the public key. This encrypted data can only be decrypted by the owner of the private key. This ensures that only the right person has access to the unencrypted data. Also, only the owner will need to keep the private key a secret since nobody else needs access to it. There is therefore no need to communicate the key to someone else.

In the image below Alice wants to encrypt another document so she can send it to Bob, without Eve being able to intercept or change it. This time she uses an asymmetric cipher and Bob's public key to encrypt it. This key is publicly available so there is no problem for Alice to get it. She then sends the encrypted document to Bob who can immediately decrypt it using his private key. Since nobody else has access to Bob's private key only Bob can decrypt the document and Eve can't.

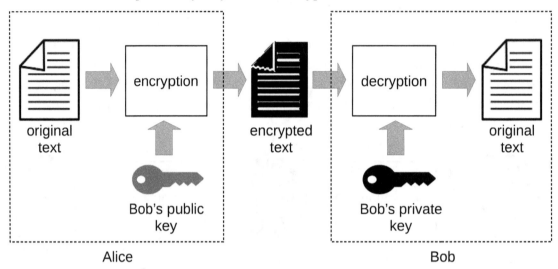

Another use of the asymmetric cipher is for the private key owner to use their private key to encrypt something. This data can then be decrypted by using the pubic key. This of course does not keep the data a secret, but it does prove the origin of the data as only the owner of the private key will have been able to encrypt that data.

Most asymmetric ciphers require more computation than most symmetric ciphers do for the same amount of data. There is also a limit to the amount of data most asymmetric ciphers can encrypt securely while most symmetric ciphers don't have this limitation. For this reason most secure protocols nowadays use an asymmetric cipher to exchange a symmetric key securely, which is then used with a symmetric cipher on the actual data to be securely transferred.

Signing

A combination of hashing and asymmetric encrypting is used to digitally sign something. To sign a file a cryptographic hash is calculated of the file's contents. That hash is then encrypted using the signer's private key. The encrypted hash is now the signature of the file. Anybody can decrypt the signature using the signer's public key and then compare the hash to one they themselves calculated of the file. If the calculated hash matches the decrypted signature then not only has the file not been tampered with, it is also proven that the file originated from the signer.

Certificates

A certificate is used to check if a public key has not been tampered with and that the owner is indeed who they say they are. A certificate contains the public key as well as the identity information of the key's owner. A certificate authority (CA) then checks the identity information and digitally signs the certificate.

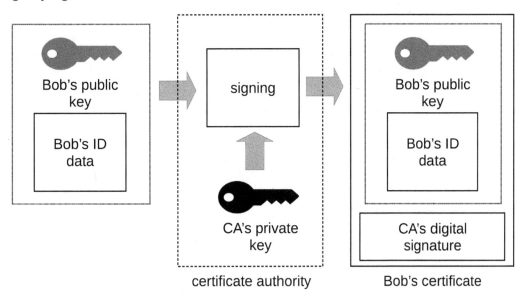

certificate authority   Bob's certificate

By checking the digital signature using the public key of the certificate authority it can be proven that the ID data and the public key on the certificate have not been tampered with and that it belongs to the owner shown on the certificate. This of course depends on the certificate authority doing a thorough job when checking the identity of the key's owner.

Sometimes a certificate can be signed by another certificate, which in turn is signed by yet another certificate, which is then finally signed by the certificate of a CA, known as the 'root CA'. This is known as a certificate chain. A chain can have any number of certificates in it, although by default the SSL library rejects any chain with more than 9 certificates in it.

Transport Layer Security

The TLS standard not only encrypts all the data so it is transported without others being able to eavesdrop on it, it also ensures that the data cannot be tampered with and it confirms the identity of the other party. Most of these things happen during the initial handshake that sets up the connection. After this handshake both sides will have the same symmetric key to be used with a symmetric cipher for the secure data transport.

At the start of communication Alice retrieves Bob's certificate. This allows Alice to check that she is indeed talking to Bob and gives her access to Bob's public key. She then randomly generates a symmetric key to use for the data transfer and encrypts it using Bob's public key. She also calculates a hash over the symmetric key and encrypts that using her own private key. She then sends Bob the encrypted key as well as the encrypted hash.

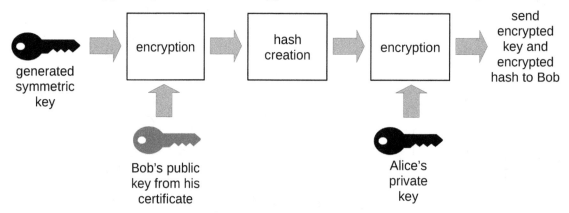

Bob receives the encrypted hash and key and retrieves Alice's certificate. He can now check that the certificate is indeed Alice's and use the public key on the certificate to decrypt the hash. Bob decrypts the symmetric key with his private key and calculates his own hash over it. If this hash is the same as the hash he decrypted from Alice then he knows that the key was indeed sent by Alice and that it has not been tampered with. Alice at the same time knows that only Bob has the private key that allows the key to be decrypted.

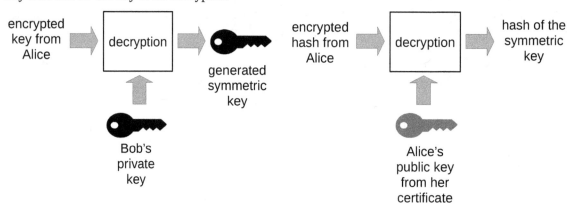

At this point both Alice and Bob now have the same symmetric key and both have checked each other's identity. They can now transfer data using a symmetric cipher and Eve will not be able to understand the message.

If Eve has access to the encrypted data and later managed to get access to Alice's or Bob's private keys then the data would still be safe. Only the key exchange used the private keys and the data itself was transferred using a randomly generated symmetric key. Access to the private keys will not give access to the symmetric key and therefore the data still can't be decrypted by Eve. Of course if Eve had the private key of Alice or Bob then she could try to impersonate the person she had obtained the key from.

The above scenario is a simplified one as it assumes that both parties use the same hashing algorithm and the same cipher. TLS allows a number of different hashing algorithms and ciphers to be used. The simplified scenario above leaves out the part of the handshake that performs the selection of the best algorithms that both sides of the connection support.

8. The AmiSSL API

Amiga support for the SSL and TLS protocols is provided by the AmiSSL library. The AmiSSL library is a port of the OpenSSL library and both libraries are actively maintained. Since AmiSSL is a direct port of the OpenSSL library most of the usage is exactly the same. This chapter will show some of the functionality of the AmiSSL/OpenSSL library, concentrating on the functions that are useful for adding TLS support to an existing sockets based networking program. The SSL library has a rather large number of functions and discussing each of them is out of the scope of this book.

The SSL library makes use of structs of which the size and contents may change between major versions of the library. To use these structs it is recommended to not access them directly but to use the library's helper functions instead. To make a distinction between normal structs and these opaque structs they will be referred to as 'objects' instead.

The header needed for these functions is: openssl/ssl.h.

Initialisation

There have been a number of different major version revisions of the OpenSSL library that were not backwards compatible with previous versions of the library. This is also true for the AmiSSL library. To deal with these changes as well as possible changes that may come in the future it is not recommended to directly open a specific version of the AmiSSL library. Also since the user may well have a newer version installed. Therefore it is recommended to open the amisslmaster.library instead. Any Amiga system that has AmiSSL installed will have the amisslmaster.library installed next to whichever versions of the main AmiSSL library that may be present on the system.

OpenAmiSSLTagList

Open the AmiSSL library.

```
long Result = OpenAmiSSLTags( long APIVersion, Tags, ... );
long Result = OpenAmiSSLTagList( long APIVersion, struct TagItem * TagList );
     D0                               D0                               A0
```

APIVersion - The minimum OpenSSL API version required. This is usually set to the value AMISSL_CURRENT_VERSION.

TagList - Standard Amiga style tag list with each tag identifying the parameter to read or change.

This function returns a 0 on success and a non-zero number on error.

There are two versions of the function. The OpenAmiSSLTagList() version takes a pointer to an array with the tags, with the last tag being TAG_END. The OpenAmiSSLTags() function takes all tags as a list of arguments, where the last argument must always be TAG_END.

Some of the supported tags:

AmiSSL_UsesOpenSSLStructs - (BOOL) OpenSSL uses structs of which the size and contents may change between versions. It is recommended to use helper functions to allocate and/or access the contents of these structs. For backwards compatibility this tag defaults to TRUE, which allows programs to allocate and modify the OpenSSL structs directly. It is recommended to set it to FALSE instead, which means that the structs can only be used via the helper functions. This will make the program less dependant on a particular OpenSSL/AmiSSL library version.

AmiSSL_GetAmiSSLBase - (struct Library **) The amisslmaster.library will store the pointer to the opened AmiSSL library into the location pointed at by the tag argument.

AmiSSL_GetAmiSSLExtBase - (struct Library **) The pointer to the extended AmiSSL library base will be stored into the location pointed at by the tag argument.

AmiSSL_SocketBase - (struct Library *) Pointer to the bsdsocket.library instance used by the program. If no networking is required (for example when using the library on files instead) then this tag can be set to NULL.

AmiSSL_ErrNoPtr – (int *) Pointer to the variable that is used by the bsdsocket.library to store its *errno* value.

Never call CloseLibrary() on any of the library base pointers acquired via OpenAmiSSLTags() or OpenAmiSSLTagList(). Only call CloseLibrary() on library pointers that were obtained by a call to the Exec OpenLibrary() function.

CloseAmiSSL

Close the AmiSSL library.

```
void    CloseAmiSSL( void );
```

Before calling the Exec CloseLibrary() function on the pointer to the amisslmaster.library the CloseAmiSSL() function must be called. This function will close all underlying libraries that were opened by the call to OpenAmiSSLTags() and free any resources allocated by these libraries.

Error checking

The SSL library uses a queue to store any errors that may occur. Since a lot of work is done in the background it is possible that a number of errors have occurred by the time the library can inform the program about it. The types of error include connectivity errors, problems with the handshake procedure as well as negative certificate verification results.

ERR_get_error

Retrieve the oldest error code from the queue.

```
unsigned long error = ERR_get_error( void );
                      D0
```

Calling this function retrieves the oldest code from the error queue and removes it from the queue. The function will return 0 when there are no more errors available in the queue. To read all codes from the queue this function can be called until it returns 0.

ERR_error_string_n

Convert an error code into a string.

```
void ERR_error_string_n( unsigned long error, char * buffer, size_t length );
                         D0                    A0               D1
```

error - The error code to be converted.

buffer - A buffer to receive the null-terminated string.

length - The size of *buffer* in bytes.

The string generated will contain a hexadecimal representation of the error code as well as the name of the library and function that caught the error. When available an additional string explaining the reason for the error will be added. The function will truncate the string when the buffer is too small.

The context

The SSL library uses a context object to store its general state. This includes configuration and setup information as well as session information. The session information is also inherited by other objects that are required later, like for example the SSL object. Usually only one context per program is required.

SSL_CTX_new

Create a new context object.

```
SSL_CTX * ctx = SSL_CTX_new( const SSL_METHOD * method );
           D0                                      A0
```

method – A method object that describes the type of context required.

If the creation of the context failed then a NULL pointer will be returned. Otherwise a pointer to the created context object will be returned. When the context object is no longer required it can be deallocated by calling the SSL_CTX_free() function.

When the object is created the SSL library will also setup the list of ciphers and prepare the session cache and setup the default options to be used with the keys and certificates.

The *method* argument is used to indicate the type of functionality required. For security reasons it is best to select a *method* that does exactly what the program needs and to never select a *method* that provides more functionality than required.

Some of the supported methods are:

> TLS_method() - To receive and create incoming and outgoing TCP connections.
>
> TLS_server_method() - To receive incoming TCP connections.
>
> TLS_client_method() - To create outgoing TCP connections.
>
> DTLS_method() - To receive / create incoming and outgoing connections based on UDP.
>
> DTLS_server_method() - The program will receive incoming connections based on UDP.
>
> DTLS_client_method() - The program will create outgoing connections based on UDP.

The methods shown above all allow for negotiation between the client and the server to establish the best protocol version to be used for the communication channel. The library also supports methods that request a particular version of the TLS standard, for example the method TLSv1_1_server_method() will create a context for a server that will only accept TLS version 1.1 connections. The use of these version bound methods is not recommended since it limits forward compatibility with newer versions of the protocols.

All method() functions return a pointer to an SSL_METHOD object, which for assembly programmers will be found in register D0 after calling the method() function.

SSL_CTX_free

Deallocate a context object.

```
      void SSL_CTX_free( SSL_CTX * ctx );
                                    A0
```

ctx - The context object to be freed.

The internal reference counter will be decremented and if it reaches zero then the object will be deallocated. All other objects that were allocated within the context will be freed as well. These objects include the list of ciphers, the session cache as well as any stored certificates and cryptographic keys.

SSL_CTX_set_default_verify_paths

Use the default paths when verifying certificates.

```
      void SSL_CTX_set_default_verify_paths( SSL_CTX * ctx );
                                                       A0
```

ctx - The context object to set.

After its creation the context object will have no search paths configured. These search paths are used to find certificates and keys when verifying a certificate. By calling this function the context is configured to use the default search paths. The default paths include the local certificate store as well as the local key store.

SSL_CTX_set_verify_depth

Set the maximum certificate chain depth allowed.

```
      void SSL_CTX_set_verify_depth( SSL_CTX * ctx, int depth );
                                               A0        D0
```

ctx - The context object to set.

depth – The maximum depth allowed.

Certificates are usually part of a chain where a certificate is signed by a certificate authority and the certificate authority's certificate could be signed by another certificate authority and so on down to a root certificate authority.

Certificates with a longer chain than specified with SSL_CTX_set_verify_depth() will fail the verification process. The default verification depth used by the SSL library is 9, which means the signed certificate itself and a chain of up to 8 authority certificates.

SSL_CTX_set_verify

Specify how to verify received certificates.

```
void SSL_CTX_set_verify( SSL_CTX * ctx, int mode, SSL_verify_cb verify_callback );
                             A0          D0                    A1
```

ctx - The context object to set.

mode - Flags that define how the verify process works.

verify_callback - A callback function to be used, or NULL if not required.

The *mode* argument is used to control how the certificate verification procedure works while the *verify_callback* function can be used to override or fine-tune the result of the procedure. How the *mode* flags function also depends on if the program acts like a server or if it acts like a client.

The function of the *mode* flags for clients:

SSL_VERIFY_NONE - The certificate received from the server will be verified but the result will not be acted upon. The handshake will continue regardless and the program can check the result of the verification by calling SSL_get_verify_result().

SSL_VERIFY_PEER - The certificate received from the server will be verified. If the verification fails then the handshake will be terminated. If no certificate is sent by the server since it is using an anonymous cipher then no verification will take place and the connection will continue. This can also be checked by calling SSL_get_verify_result().

The function of the *mode* flags for servers:

SSL_VERIFY_NONE - Do not send a certificate to the client. This then means that the client will not send a certificate back either.

SSL_VERIFY_PEER - Request a certificate from the client. If the client returns a certificate then verify it. If the verification fails then the handshake is terminated.

SSL_VERIFY_FAIL_IF_NO_PEER_CERT - If the client did not return a certificate upon requesting one then the handshake is terminated. This mode flag must be used together with the SSL_VERIFY_PEER flag.

SSL_VERIFY_CLIENT_ONCE - Only request the client certificate at the initial handshake. Do not request it again if a renegotiation occurs. This mode flag must be used together with the SSL_VERIFY_PEER flag.

If a pointer to the verification callback was provided then the library will always call the callback function after it has verified the received certificate. This gives the program the opportunity to perform its own checks and overrule the result of the library.

The signature of the callback function is as follows:

```
int (*SSL_verify_cb)( int preverify_ok, X509_STORE_CTX * x509_ctx );
```

preverify_ok – It is set to 0 if the certificate failed its verification, otherwise it is set to 1.

x509_ctx - The x509 store context object that can be used to query the certificate.

The callback returns an integer with the same semantics as the *preverify_ok* argument; when set to 0 the verification process is regarded as having failed and the handshake will be terminated. When the callback returns 1 the verification was successful and the handshake is continued. The callback function will be called for every certificate in the chain.

When the *verify_callback* argument is set to NULL the default callback is used which directly returns the preverify_ok value.

SSL_CTX_use_certificate_file

Specify the certificate to use.

```
int Result = SSL_CTX_use_certificate_file( SSL_CTX * ctx,
    D0                                         A0
                                     const char * file, int type );
                                                  A1         D0
```

ctx - The context object to load the certificate to.

file - The path to the file containing the certificate.

type - The file format of the certificate file.

The function reads the first certificate from the file and stores it in the context object. To load a complete certificate chain the function SSL_CTX_use_certificate_chain_file() should be used. The function will return 1 on success. Other values will indicate that an error occurred. The reason for the error can be found in the error queue.

The following file formats are supported by the *type* argument:

SSL_FILETYPE_PEM - The file is in the PEM format.

SSL_FILETYPE_ASN1 - The file is in the ASN.1 format.

Calling this function before SSL_CTX_use_PrivateKey_file() allows the library to compare the private key with the public key of the certificate.

SSL_CTX_use_certificate_chain_file

Specify a certificate chain to use.

```
int Result = SSL_CTX_use_certificate_chain_file( SSL_CTX * ctx, const char* file );
    D0                                                         A0              A1
```

ctx - The context object to load the certificate to.

file - The path to the file containing the certificate chain.

The function reads the certificate chain from the file, which must be in PEM format, and stores it in the context object. The function will return 1 on success. Other values will indicate that an error occurred. The reason for the error can be found in the error queue.

SSL_CTX_use_PrivateKey_file

Specify the private key to use.

```
int Result = SSL_CTX_use_PrivateKey_file( SSL_CTX * ctx,
    D0                                               A0
                                          const char * file, int type );
                                                       A1          D0
```

ctx - The context object to load the private key to.

file - The path to the file containing the private key.

type - The file format of the private key file.

The function reads the private key from the file and stores it in the context object. The function returns 1 on success. Other values indicate an error. The reason for the error can be found in the error queue.

The following file formats are supported by the *type* argument:

SSL_FILETYPE_PEM - The file is in the PEM format.

SSL_FILETYPE_ASN1 - The file is in the ASN.1 format.

It is recommended to call this function after calling the SSL_CTX_use_certificate_file() function or the SSL_CTX_use_certificate_chain_file() function since it allows the library to compare the private key with the public key of the certificate (chain).

SSL/TLS communication

The library provides an SSL object to control the SSL/TLS part of the connection. This object is used in a similar fashion as the socket descriptor is used for a standard network connection. When the SSL object is created it will inherit its session information from the context object.

SSL_new

Create the SSL object.

```
SSL * ssl = SSL_new( SSL_CTX * ctx );
    D0                      A0
```

ctx - The context object from which to create the SSL object.

In case of an error the function will return NULL and the reason for the failure will be stored in the error queue. On success the function will return a pointer to the created SSL object. The object must be freed by calling SSL_free() when no longer needed.

SSL_free

Free the SSL object.

```
void SSL_free( SSL * ssl );
                      A0
```

ssl - The SSL object to be freed.

The internal reference counter will be decremented and if it reaches zero then the SSL object will be deallocated including any objects that were internally allocated by the SSL object.

SSL_set_fd

Associate a socket descriptor with the SSL object.

```
int result = SSL_set_fd( SSL * ssl, int sd );
    D0                         A0         D0
```

ssl - The SSL object to be used.

sd - The descriptor of the socket used for the connection.

In case of an error the function will return 0 and the reason for the failure will be stored in the error queue. On success the function will return a value of 1.

In the Unix/Linux world a socket descriptor is just another file descriptor, which is why the OpenSSL function is called SSL_set_fd() and not SSL_set_sd() for example. The AmiSSL library aims to stay as close to OpenSSL as possible and kept the name as-is for compatibility reasons.

SSL_get_error

Get the reason for an SSL I/O failure.

```
int Result = SSL_get_error( const SSL * ssl, int ret );
    D0                                    A0        D0
```

ssl - The SSL object to be used.

ret - The return value of the function that indicated the error.

This function will return an error code that indicates the reason for the previous function call's failure. The SSL_get_error() function must always be called directly after the function indicating the failure, with no other SSL library functions being called by the program in the mean time.

Some of the values that SSL_get_error() may return:

SSL_ERROR_NONE - The SSL operation has completed successfully.

SSL_ERROR_ZERO_RETURN - The SSL connection has been closed. This value indicates that the SSL part of the connection has been closed cleanly. This does not necessarily indicate that the connection on the socket has been closed as well.

SSL_ERROR_WANT_READ - Not necessarily an error. The read operation did not complete and must be called again in order to complete. Calling again does not guarantee that the operation will complete during this second call; it may be required to call the operation a number of times before it completes.

SSL_ERROR_WANT_WRITE – Not necessarily an error. The write operation did not complete and must be called again in order to complete. Calling again does not guarantee that the operation will complete during this second call; it may be required to call the operation a number of times before it completes.

SSL_ERROR_SYSCALL - An I/O error was detected. The error queue of the SSL library may contain more information. If there is no more information then the value of the *ret* argument can be inspected, where 0 means that the underlying connection has disconnected unexpectedly. A value of -1 means that there was a socket error and that the socket's *errno* variable needs to be inspected to find out the actual error.

SSL_ERROR_SSL - A protocol error occurred or some other failure within the SSL library. Check the error queue for more information on the error.

SSL_set_tlsext_host_name

Set the name of the host to connect to.

```
int result = SSL_set_tlsext_host_name( SSL * ssl, const char * name );
```

ssl - The SSL object to be used.

name - The name of the host.

On success the function will return a value of 1, otherwise it will return a 0. The function is a macro that calls the SSL_ctrl() function. This macro is not available for assembly language programs which will need to use the SSL_ctrl() function instead.

Most web servers on the Internet serve more than one website/host and each website/host will need its own certificate. Calling SSL_set_tlsext_host_name() with the name of the website/host the program wants to connect to allows the server to use the correct certificate.

This function is only used by programs acting as clients and will be ignored by the SSL library when acting as a server.

SSL_set_mode

Set an SSL mode of operation.

```
long modes = SSL_set_mode( SSL * ssl, long mode );
```

ssl - The SSL object to be used.

mode – A mask of the required mode(s) of operation to be set.

The function adds the new mode to the modes already set and returns the bitmask of all modes that are now set. The function is a macro that calls the SSL_ctrl() function. This macro is not available for assembly language programs which will need to use the SSL_ctrl() function instead.

Each mode value sets a bit in a bitmask and the values can therefore be combined with bitwise OR when multiple modes need to be enabled.

The following modes are available:

> SSL_MODE_AUTO_RETRY - By default the library interrupts SSL_read() and SSL_write() calls when a renegotiation is required. By setting this mode flag the library will perform the renegotiation in the background. This will be transparent to the program, unless the renegotiation fails for some reason. Then the read/write call will be interrupted with an appropriate error.

SSL_MODE_ENABLE_PARTIAL_WRITE - By default a successful SSL_write() using a blocking socket will only return after all bytes have been sent. Setting this mode allows SSL_write() to return after only a part of the data has been sent successfully. To send the rest of the data the SSL_write() function must be called again with only the unsent data in the buffer.

SSL_MODE_ACCEPT_MOVING_WRITE_BUFFER - By default a retry of SSL_write() must happen with the same arguments as the original call to SSL_write(). When this mode is set the data pointer can be changed, as long as it points to a buffer that contains the same data as used by the original SSL_write() call.

SSL_MODE_RELEASE_BUFFERS - Release all unused buffers. Depending on the number of buffers these may not actually be released back to the system but instead added to the library's internal list of buffers ready to be used again.

SSL_clear_mode

Clear an SSL mode of operation.

```
long modes = SSL_clear_mode( SSL * ssl, long mode );
```

ssl - The SSL object to be used.

mode - A mask of the mode(s) of operation to be cleared.

The function removes the specified mode(s) from the modes already set and returns the bitmask of all modes that are still set. The function is a macro that calls the SSL_ctrl() function. This macro is not available for assembly programs which will need to use the SSL_ctrl() function instead.

Please see SSL_set_mode() for more information on the available modes.

SSL_ctrl

Control behaviour of the SSL object.

```
int result = SSL_ctrl( SSL * ssl, int cmd, long larg, void * parg );
    D0                    A0       D0,    D1          A1
```

ssl - The SSL object to be used.

cmd - The command for the SSL object.

larg – An integer argument used by the command.

parg – A pointer argument used by the command.

The SSL_ctrl() function is used to change the settings of the SSL object. The return value of the function depends on the *cmd* argument.

For C programs it is not recommended to call this function directly, but to use the helper macros like SSL_set_mode(), SSL_clear_mode() and SSL_set_tlsext_host_name() instead.

Some of the supported commands:

> SSL_CTRL_SET_TLSEXT_HOSTNAME – Set the name of the host to connect to. The *larg* argument needs to be set to TLSEXT_NAMETYPE_host_name, the *parg* argument needs to point to the string with the host name. The return value will be 1 for success and 0 for failure. See the SSL_set_tlsext_host_name() function for more information.

> SSL_CTRL_MODE – Set the mode of the SSL object. The *larg* argument needs to contain a mask of the mode(s) to be added, the *parg* argument needs to be NULL. The return value will be a bitmask of the modes that are now active. See the SSL_set_mode() function for more information.

> SSL_CTRL_CLEAR_MODE – Clear mode(s) from the SSL object. The *larg* argument needs to contain a mask of the mode(s) to be removed, the *parg* argument needs to be NULL. The return value will be a bitmask of the modes that are now active. See the SSL_clear_mode() function for more information.

SSL_connect

Initiate the handshake process with a server.

```
int result = SSL_connect( SSL * ssl );
    D0                          A0
```

ssl - The SSL object to be used.

On success the function will return a value of 1. If the handshake did not fail but was terminated by either end (for example due to incompatible ciphers or certificate verification issues) then the function will return 2. If there was a protocol failure then the function will return 3. When the function returns 2 or 3 the reason for the failure will be returned by SSL_get_error().

SSL_connect() is used by the client to start the SSL/TLS handshake with the server. It expects that the socket that was associated via a call to SSL_set_fd() to have already been successfully connected to the server. If the socket used is a blocking socket then the SSL_connect() function will block until the handshake is either finished or has been terminated.

When used with a non-blocking socket the SSL_connect() call will return immediately. If the SSL/TLS handshake has not finished yet then the function will return -1 and the value returned by SSL_get_error() will either be SSL_ERROR_WANT_READ or SSL_ERROR_WANT_WRITE. These values means that internally the SSL library needs to wait for another read or write respectively. The socket's asynchronous events will indicate when that read or write has happened and at that point the SSL_connect() function will need to be called again to continue the handshake. This process may need to be repeated a couple of times until the function not longer returns -1.

SSL_accept

Answer the handshake process initiated by a client.

```
int result = SSL_accept( SSL * ssl );
    D0                           A0
```

ssl - The SSL object to be used.

On success the function will return a value of 1. If the handshake did not fail but was terminated by either end (for example due to incompatible ciphers or certificate verification issues) then the function will return 2. If there was a protocol failure then the function will return 3. When the function returns 2 or 3 the reason for the failure will be returned by SSL_get_error().

SSL_accept() is used by the server to receive the start of the SSL/TLS handshake from a client. It expects that the socket that was associated via a call to SSL_set_fd() to be a new socket from the socket library's accept() function. If the socket used is a blocking socket then the SSL_accept() function will block until the handshake is either finished or has been terminated.

When used on a non-blocking socket the SSL_accept() call will return immediately. If the SSL/TLS handshake has not finished yet then the function will return -1 and the value returned by SSL_get_error() will be either SSL_ERROR_WANT_READ or SSL_ERROR_WANT_WRITE. These values means that internally the SSL library needs to wait for another read or write respectively. The socket's asynchronous events will indicate when that read or write has happened and at that point the SSL_accept() function will need to be called again to continue the handshake. This process may need to be repeated a couple of times until the function not longer returns -1.

SSL_get_verify_result

Get the result of the certificate verification process.

```
long result = SSL_get_verify_result( const SSL * ssl );
    D0                                          A0
```

ssl - The SSL object to be used.

The function will return the outcome of the verification process of the peer's certificate.

Some of the possible return values are:

X509_V_OK - No problems were detected with the certificate, or none was presented.

X509_V_ERR_CERT_REVOKED - The certificate has been revoked.

X509_V_ERR_CERT_HAS_EXPIRED - The notAfter date on the certificate is in the past.

X509_V_ERR_CERT_NOT_YET_VALID - The certificate has a notBefore date that is still in the future.

X509_V_ERR_CERT_SIGNATURE_FAILURE – The signature is not valid.

X509_V_ERR_SELF_SIGNED_CERT_IN_CHAIN – One or more of the certificates in the chain are self-signed and the root certificate can't be found in the local store.

X509_V_ERR_DEPTH_ZERO_SELF_SIGNED_CERT - The certificate itself is self signed and is not one of the trusted certificates in the local store.

X509_V_ERR_CERT_CHAIN_TOO_LONG – Too many certificates in the chain. See also the SSL_CTX_set_verify_depth() function.

Please note that this function will also indicate success if the peer did not present a certificate. It is therefore important to use the X509 functions (in a later section) to check that there was indeed a certificate presented by the peer.

SSL_write

Send data over the encrypted part of the connection.

```
int result = SSL_write( SSL * ssl, const void * data, int size );
     D0                       A0               A1          D0
```

ssl - The SSL object to be used.

data - Pointer to the data to be sent.

size - Size of the data in bytes.

Upon success this function will return the number of bytes written. When the function returns 0 nothing was written, most likely since the connection is no longer there. The actual reason can be found from SSL_get_error(). The function will return a negative value when an error has occurred. Again the reason can be found by calling SSL_get_error().

On a blocking socket the function will only return after the operation has finished, an error has occurred or if a renegotiation is required.

The SSL_write() call will return immediately when used with a non-blocking socket. If the data could not be written immediately then the SSL_get_error() function will return a value of SSL_ERROR_WANT_WRITE.

If a renegotiation is required then the function will also return and the SSL_get_error() function will return SSL_ERROR_WANT_READ. Use the SSL_MODE_AUTO_RETRY flag with the SSL_set_mode() function to change this behaviour.

If the SSL_write() function must be called again because of he SSL_get_error() function returning SSL_ERROR_WANT_READ or SSL_ERROR_WANT_WRITE then this must be done using the same arguments as the original call to SSL_write().

SSL_read

Receive data from the encrypted part of the connection.

```
int result = SSL_read( SSL * ssl, void * buffer, int size );
      D0                    A0          A1          D0
```

ssl - The SSL object to be used.

buffer - Pointer to the buffer to place the received data in.

size - Size of the buffer in bytes.

When successful SSL_read() will return the number of bytes read. When the function returns 0 nothing was read, most likely since the connection is no longer there. The actual reason can be found from SSL_get_error(). The function will return a negative value when an error has occurred, the reason can be found with a call to SSL_get_error() too.

The SSL protocol uses records of a size that is not related to the TCP segment size to communicate over the secure channel. The SSL_read() function can only deliver data after a complete record has been received and decrypted. This may require reading multiple segments from the network socket. The SSL_read() function will only process one record at the time and never produce more data than one record can contain.

On a blocking socket the function will only return if there is data to be read, an error has occurred or if a renegotiation is required. Otherwise it will block until any of these conditions occur.

The SSL_read() call will return immediately when used with a non-blocking socket. If there is no data to be read then SSL_get_error() will return either the value SSL_ERROR_WANT_READ or the value SSL_ERROR_WANT_WRITE.

If a renegotiation is required then the function will also return and the SSL_get_error() function will return SSL_ERROR_WANT_READ. Use the SSL_MODE_AUTO_RETRY flag with the SSL_set_mode() function to change this behaviour.

If the SSL_read() function must be called again because of the SSL_get_error() function returning SSL_ERROR_WANT_READ or SSL_ERROR_WANT_WRITE then this must be done using the same arguments as the original call to SSL_read().

SSL_shutdown

Shut down the SSL part of a connection.

```
int result = SSL_shutdown( SSL * ssl );
      D0                          A0
```

ssl - The SSL object to be used.

The function returns a value of 1 when the shutdown handshake with the remote system has successfully ended. If it returns a value of 2 then then the shutdown handshake has not yet finished and the function can be called again. A return value of 3 and negative return values both indicate an error of which the reason can be obtained from SSL_get_error().

For blocking sockets the call to SSL_shutdown() will block until the operation has completed. For non-blocking sockets the first call to SSL_shutdown() will start the process and immediately return with a value of 0. This value indicates that the shutdown process is still ongoing. To check the status of the shutdown process SSL_shutdown() can be called again until it returns a non-zero value, at which point the shutdown process has completed.

If the SSL_shutdown() function returns 2 and on calling again indicates an error with SSL_get_error() returning SSL_ERROR_SYSCALL then this error can be safely ignored. Call the function again until either the shutdown handshake finishes or a different error occurs.

Certificates

The certificates are stored and transferred in the X509 format. The SSL library provides an X509 object that can be used to access the information stored in a certificate through a number of helper functions. The X509 object can then be used for additional validity checks as well as providing additional information about the certificate to the user, like the name of the certificate authority that signed the certificate.

The header needed for these functions is: openssl/x509.h

SSL_get1_peer_certificate

Get the certificate presented by the peer.

```
X509 * x509 = SSL_get1_peer_certificate( const SSL * ssl );
      D0                                           A0
```

ssl - The SSL object used for the connection.

This function returns a pointer to an X509 object that contains the certificate that was presented by the peer. If no certificate was presented then the function will return NULL.

After use the X509 object must be freed by calling X509_free().

X509_free

Free an X509 object.

```
void X509_free( X509 * x509 );
                         A0
```

x509 - The X509 object to be freed.

The X509 object uses an internal reference counter. This function decrements the counter and will free the object when the counter reaches a value of zero.

X509_cmp_time

Compare two timestamps.

```
int result = X509_cmp_time( const ASN1_TIME * asn1_time, time_t * in_tm );
    D0                                        A0                  A1
```

asn1_time - A timestamp in ASN.1 format (the format used by the X509 standard).

in_tm - A timestamp in the format of the operating system.

The function will return -1 when *asn1_time* is earlier than (or the same as) *in_tm*. When *asn1_time* is later than *in_tm* the function will return 1. If there is an error then the function will return 0.

X509_cmp_current_time

Compare a timestamp with the current time.

```
int result = X509_cmp_current_time( const ASN1_TIME * asn1_time );
    D0                                                A0
```

asn1_time - A timestamp in ASN.1 format (the format used by the X509 standard).

The function returns -1 when *asn1_time* is in the past or is equal to the current time. When *asn1_time* is in the future the function will return 1. If there is an error then then it will return 0.

X509_get_issuer_name

Get the issuer of the certificate.

```
X509_NAME * name = X509_get_issuer_name( const X509 * x509 );
            D0                                          A0
```

x509 - The X509 certificate object to get the issuer of.

This function will return a pointer to an X509_NAME object with name of the issuer of the certificate. This object is internal to the X509 object and should not be freed. The SSL library provides helper functions to access the information in the X509_NAME object, see for example the X509_NAME_oneline() function later in this section.

X509_get_subject_name

Get the subject of the certificate.

```
X509_NAME * name = X509_get_subject_name( const X509 * x509 );
            D0                                           A0
```

x509 - The X509 certificate object to get the subject of.

This function will return a pointer to an X509_NAME object with the subject of the certificate. This object is internal to the X509 object and should not be freed. The SSL library provides functions to access the information in the X509_NAME object, like the X509_NAME_oneline() directly below.

X509_NAME_oneline

Get the X509_NAME contents as a single line string.

```
char * string = X509_NAME_oneline( X509_NAME * name, char * buffer, int size );
       D0                                       A0           A1         D0
```

name - The X509_NAME object to get the contents of.

buffer – Pointer to a buffer to receive the string or NULL.

size - Size of *buffer* in bytes.

The function will copy as many characters as will fit into the buffer and zero terminate it. The pointer returned by the function is the same pointer as was passed for the buffer argument.

If NULL is passed for the *buffer* argument then the X509_NAME_oneline function will dynamically allocate a buffer for the string and return the pointer to it. When no longer required this buffer must be freed with OPENSSL_free().

X509_STORE_CTX_get_current_cert

Get the current certificate from the store.

```
X509 * x509 = X509_STORE_CTX_get_current_cert( const X509_STORE_CTX * x509_ctx );
       D0                                                                    A0
```

x509_ctx - The certificate store context object.

This function returns a pointer to an X509 object that contains the certificate that was presented by the peer. If there is no current certificate then the function will return NULL, which can happen if the peer did not offer a certificate during the handshake. After use the X509 object must be freed by calling X509_free().

Usually this function is called from the certificate verification callback function (see the previous section on SSL_CTX_set_verify()). The callback function receives a pointer to the certificate store context object as one of its arguments.

X509_STORE_CTX_get_error

Get the certificate verification error code.

```
int error = X509_STORE_CTX_get_error( const X509_STORE_CTX * x509_ctx );
    D0                                                              A0
```

x509_ctx - The certificate store context object.

The function will return the error code related to the certificate verification error, or X509_V_OK if there was no error. Please note that if the peer did not offer a certificate then the function will also return the X509_V_OK value.

Some of the possible return values are:

X509_V_OK - No problems were detected with the certificate, or none was presented.

X509_V_ERR_CERT_REVOKED - The certificate has been revoked.

X509_V_ERR_CERT_HAS_EXPIRED - The notAfter date on the certificate is in the past.

X509_V_ERR_CERT_NOT_YET_VALID - The certificate has a notBefore date that is still in the future.

X509_V_ERR_CERT_SIGNATURE_FAILURE – The signature is not valid.

X509_V_ERR_SELF_SIGNED_CERT_IN_CHAIN – One or more of the certificates in the chain are self-signed and the root certificate can't be found in the local store.

X509_V_ERR_DEPTH_ZERO_SELF_SIGNED_CERT - The certificate itself is self signed and is not one of the trusted certificates in the local store.

X509_V_ERR_CERT_CHAIN_TOO_LONG – Too many certificates in the chain. See also the SSL_CTX_set_verify_depth() function.

Usually this function is called from the certificate verification callback function (see the previous section on SSL_CTX_set_verify()). The callback function receives a pointer to the certificate store context object as one of its arguments.

X509_verify_cert_error_string

Convert a verification error into a string.

```
const char * string = X509_verify_cert_error_string( long error );
               D0                                            D0
```

error - The error code to be converted.

The return value is a pointer to a null-terminated string. If the error code is invalid then a string will be returned showing just the error number that was passed with the *error* argument.

Ciphers

During the SSL/TLS handshake the two sides of the connection will negotiate with each other to select the best cipher to use. The following functions can be used to find out which cipher was selected to be used for the secure part of the connection.

SSL_get_pending_cipher

Get the cipher for the coming session.

```
const SSL_CIPHER * cipher = SSL_get_pending_cipher( const SSL * ssl );
                      D0                                          A0
```

ssl - The SSL object used for the connection.

This function will return a pointer to an SSL_CIPHER object for the cipher that will be used when the secure connection has been established. If no cipher has been negotiated (yet) then the function will return a NULL pointer.

This function can be used to obtain cipher information while the secure connection has not yet been setup, like during the handshake for example. The cipher object will contain information regarding the cipher that was negotiated.

SSL_get_current_cipher

Get the cipher for the current session.

```
const SSL_CIPHER * cipher = SSL_get_current_cipher( const SSL * ssl );
                    D0                                           A0
```

ssl - The SSL object used for the connection.

This function will return a pointer to a cipher object if a secure connection has been established. Or it will return NULL when there is no secure connection active. The cipher object will contain information regarding the cipher that is currently used for the connection.

SSL_CIPHER_get_name

Get a string with the name of the cipher.

```
const char * name = SSL_CIPHER_get_name( const SSL_CIPHER * cipher );
                D0                                       A0
```

cipher - The cipher object to get the name from.

This function will return a human readable read-only string with the name of the cipher. If the pointer to the cipher object is NULL then the string returned will be "(NONE)".

9. AmiSSL in C

This chapter goes into the practical side of using AmiSSL/OpenSSL in programs written in C.

The three AmiSSL examples are based on the TCP examples from the 'Sockets in C' chapter. This chapter will concentrate on the SSL/TLS parts that were added and skip the parts that have already been highlighted previously. One of the TCP examples uses non-blocking sockets, the other two of the SSL examples use blocking sockets. Using blocking sockets simplifies the examples and makes the SSL/TLS parts much easier to follow.

For brevity the code shown here has most of the error recovery removed, the full source in the download will have most of this implemented. There will therefore be some differences between the code here in the book and the source code in the download.

All these examples are meant to be run from the CLI/Shell and not from the Workbench. This is since the examples use the CLI/Shell window to show progress by using printing to the window.

Setting up

Additional to the setup required for the bsdsocket.library (as shown in a previous chapter) there is now also setup required for the SSL library. With VBCC the bsdsocket.library is opened automatically due to the -lauto linker flag, but the SSL libraries need to be opened by the program code itself for VBCC as well as GCC. The requested stack size is increased from 10240 bytes for the previous examples to 20480 bytes for these SSL examples.

Opening the library

AmiSSL is a port of the OpenSSL library and each time the OpenSSL library receives an update a new version of AmiSSL is released shortly after. AmiSSL allows multiple versions of the SSL library to be installed on the same system. A program should therefore only open the amisslmaster.library and let the library help with opening the best suitable SSL library that is installed on the system. The Exec OpenLibrary() function is used to open the master library and obtain a pointer to it.

```
struct Library * AmiSSLMasterBase;
AmiSSLMasterBase = OpenLibrary( "amisslmaster.library", AMISSLMASTER_MIN_VERSION );
if ( !AmiSSLMasterBase )
{
    // AmiSSL is probably not installed on the system.
}
```

The master library can now be used to open the SSL library itself. The SSL library needs to have access to the bsdsocket.library and also to the *ErrNo* variable. At the same time it needs to populate the pointers to library structs called AmiSSLBase and AmiSSLExtBase. This can all be done with a single call to the OpenAmiSSLTags() function.

```
OpenAmiSSLTags( AMISSL_CURRENT_VERSION,
        AmiSSL_UsesOpenSSLStructs, FALSE,
        AmiSSL_GetAmiSSLBase, &AmiSSLBase,
        AmiSSL_GetAmiSSLExtBase, &AmiSSLExtBase,
        AmiSSL_SocketBase, SocketBase,
        AmiSSL_ErrNoPtr, &ErrNo,
        TAG_END );
```

The names of the library pointers AmiSSLMasterBase, AmiSSLBase and AmiSSLExtBase can not be changed; the header files of the AmiSSL library depend on these pointers to have exactly these names. Changing any of these pointer names will lead to linker errors.

Closing the library

While the program was running the SSL library may have allocated quite a number of structures and caches in memory. These need to be freed by calling the CloseAmiSSL() function before the master library is closed with the Exec CloseLibrary() function.

```
CloseAmiSSL();
CloseLibrary( AmiSSLMasterBase );
```

Getting error code information

The functions of the SSL library may indicate that an error has occurred. When this happens the ERR_get_error() function of the SSL library can be used to get the code for the error. The ERR_error_string_n() function can then be used to convert the code into a human readable string that can be shown to the user. This string is obtained as follows:

```
char Buffer[ 256 ];
ERR_error_string_n( ERR_get_error(), Buffer, 256 );
```

The SSL-Client example

This example is based on the TCP-Connect example but uses a blocking socket instead. It makes a connection to port 443, the standard port for a secure web server, and makes a simple GET request for the root page on the server. After this it will wait for the data that is being sent by the server and disconnect when everything has been received.

The example takes either the IP address or the hostname of the server to connect to as an argument.

Preparing the library

The SSL library uses a context object to store its main state. This example will act as a client and creates a new context object intended for use by clients.

```
SSL_CTX * pCtx = SSL_CTX_new( TLS_client_method() );
if ( !pCtx )
{
    // This is an error, gracefully terminate.
}
```

The context object is then used to setup the verification of the certificate that the server is going to send during the initiation handshake. The function SSL_CTX_set_default_verify_paths() is called to make the SSL library use the default locations to look for the root certificates on the system. Without this call the library will not look anywhere.

```
SSL_CTX_set_default_verify_paths( pCtx );
SSL_CTX_set_verify( pCtx, SSL_VERIFY_PEER |
                        SSL_VERIFY_FAIL_IF_NO_PEER_CERT, verify_cb );
```

The call to SSL_CTX_set_verify() specifies how the library should verify the certificate from the server and also provides a pointer to the callback function. This callback function will be called after the library has done its verification on a certificate and can be used to overrule the result of the verification. The callback function itself will be shown later in its own section.

For each connection a separate SSL object is required. This object is created with the SSL_new() function, which takes the context object as an argument. After that the SSL object is used to setup parameters for the upcoming connection.

```
SSL * pSSL = SSL_new( pCtx );
if ( !pSSL )
{
    // This is an error, gracefully terminate.
}
```

The example will use a SOCK_STREAM type socket to connect to the server and then the SSL library will be used for the TLS parts of the connection. To be able to do this the SSL library will need access to the socket that will be used. This is done with the SSL_set_fd() function that takes the socket descriptor as its argument.

```
SSL_set_fd( pSSL, Socket );
```

The SSL_set_mode() function is used to enable the auto retry mode so that the SSL library will take care of renegotiation should this be required.

```
SSL_set_mode( pSSL, SSL_MODE_AUTO_RETRY );
```

The SSL_set_tlsext_host_name() function sets the hostname of the server that the client is going to connect to. This is important when connecting to a server that hosts multiple sites as it informs the server which site's certificate is being requested.

```
SSL_set_tlsext_host_name( pSSL, pName );
```

The GET request will also contain the hostname, but that is only sent after all the SSL handshaking has been done, and a certificate has been sent. The SSL_set_tlsext_host_name() function ensures that the server already knows the correct hostname before it sends the certificate.

Starting the handshake

The example uses blocking sockets, which means that the socket is connected to the server as soon as the connect() function returns with a success result. The handshake process is started with a call to the SSL_connect() function. Due to the blocking socket this function will only return when the handshake has either successfully finished or has been terminated with an error.

When the SSL_connect() function returns with an error no secure channel will have been setup. The HTTPS protocol does not allow for unsecure communication between the client and the server, so in that case the client will close the socket and terminate gracefully.

```
Result = SSL_connect( pSSL );
if ( Result < 0 )
{
    // This is an error, check ERR_get_error() for more information
}
```

A validation failure of the server's certificate is one reason for the call to return an error, but failing the handshake process due to incompatible algorithms like ciphers or key exchange algorithms is also possible.

The validation callback

While the handshake is being performed the server will send its certificate chain. Each certificate in the chain will be validated individually and after each validation the callback function is called. The validation callback will be called as many times as there are certificates in the chain.

The callback function in the example will check the verification error if the verification failed. If the error was caused by the certificate being only self-signed then the callback will return a value of 1 to indicate that the certificate is allowed. For a real world application that could allow a man-in-the-middle (MITM) attack, which for this example is less of an issue.

The *PreverifyOK* argument of the callback will have value of 0 when the verification by the SSL library failed and will have a value of 1 when the verification was successful. The library refers to this as the 'pre' verification as the callback function can be used to overrule the result and has the last say in the matter.

```
static int verify_cb( int PreverifyOK, X509_STORE_CTX * pStoreCtx )
{
    if ( !PreverifyOK )
    {
        int Err = X509_STORE_CTX_get_error( pStoreCtx );
        if ( Err == X509_V_ERR_DEPTH_ZERO_SELF_SIGNED_CERT )
        {
            PreverifyOK = 1; // Allow self-signed certificates
        }
        else
        {
            const char * pStr = X509_verify_cert_error_string( Err );
            printf( "Certificate verification failed (%s)\n", pStr );
        }
    }
    return PreverifyOK;
}
```

The example will also print out some certificate information when the verification is successful.

Data transfer

The secure channel over the TCP connection with the server has been established when the SSL_connect() function returns with a successful result. Now all data being sent and received will be fully encrypted and cannot be peeked at by a 3rd party.

Instead of the send() function of the socket library all data now needs to be transmitted with the SSL_write() function of the SSL library. This function will encrypt the data and send it using the socket that was associated with the SSL object earlier.

A simple GET request string was created and stored in the *RequestStr* buffer previously and is sent to the server as follows:

```
int BytesDone = SSL_write( pSSL, RequestStr, strlen( RequestStr ) );
if ( BytesDone < 0 )
{
    // This is an error, check ERR_get_error() for more information
}
```

Similarly the data that is being returned by the server is not read with the socket library's recv() function but with SSL_read() instead. The example keeps calling SSL_read() until a negative value or a value of 0 is returned. A negative value indicates an error while a value of 0 indicates that the server wants to shutdown the connection.

```
char Buffer[ 2048 ];
int BytesRead = 0;
while ( (BytesRead = SSL_read( pSSL, Buffer, 2047 )) > 0 )
{
    // Process the data that was read
}
```

Shutting down

When the TLS part of the connection is no longer required the SSL_shutdown() function can be called. This starts the shutdown handshake and terminates secure channel in a graceful way.

```
SSL_shutdown( pSSL );
```

When the call returns the handshake has finished, but the TCP connection is still there as a normal unencrypted connection. This connection can now be ended with a call to shutdown() using an argument with a value of 2 to indicate that nothing will be sent nor received via this connection.

Cleaning up

All that needs to be done to clean up is to call CloseSocket() with the socket descriptor as its argument and to free the two SSL library objects that were used.

```
CloseSocket( Socket );
SSL_free( pSSL );
SSL_CTX_free( pCtx );
```

At this point the SSL library can be closed as described earlier in this chapter.

The SSL-Client-NB example

This example is similar to the SSL-Client example but uses a non-blocking socket instead. There are a lot of similarities between this example and the previous one, like the setup of the SSL libraries and the creation of the Context and SSL objects. These have been omitted in this section, which will concentrate on the parts that are different.

The example makes a connection to port 443, the standard port for a secure web server, and makes a simple GET request for the root page on the server. After this it will wait for the data that is being sent by the server and disconnect when everything has been received.

The example takes either the IP address or the hostname of the server to connect to as an argument.

Checking for errors

When using a non-blocking socket many SSL library functions may return an error that, when checked with a call to SSL_get_error(), turns out to be merely an indication that the call is in progress and that another call needs to be made later. To check for this situation a new error checking function was added to the example.

```
int HasSSLError( SSL * pSSL, int ReturnValue, const char * pMsg )
{
    int Error = SSL_get_error( pSSL, ReturnValue );
    switch ( Error )
    {
        case SSL_ERROR_WANT_READ :
            printf( "SSL_ERROR_WANT_READ " );
            return 0;

        case SSL_ERROR_WANT_WRITE :
            printf( "SSL_ERROR_WANT_WRITE " );
            return 0;
    }
    SSLError( pMsg );

    return 1;
}
```

The function will return 0 if the result is not an error but is an SSL_ERROR_WANT_READ or an SSL_ERROR_WANT_WRITE instead. If the result is an error then the function will print the error and return a value of 1.

Channel status

With the blocking socket there was no need to track the status of the secure channel. For example when the call to SSL_connect() returned there was either an error or the status of the secure channel had changed from idle to connected.

With a non-blocking socket the SSL_connect() function needs to be called multiple times. The first call will start the handshake process and then the function needs to be called again to check if the handshake ended, and if it has, if it ended successfully. Sometimes this means that the SSL_connect() function needs to be called a number of times before the TLS part of the connection has been successfully established.

To keep track of the status of the secure channel an enum is introduced that is used to reflect at what stage the channel currently is.

```
enum SSLStatus { IDLE, CONNECTING, CONNECTED };
```

Connecting

When the socket's connection to the server has been established the FD_CONNECT event is signalled by the socket library. This event is signalled only once per connection and is used to change the channel status from IDLE to CONNECTING.

```
if ( EventMask & FD_CONNECT )
{
    printf( "FD_CONNECT\n" );
    SSLStatus = CONNECTING;
}
```

The SSL library will use the socket to communicate the handshake data with the server. This will then cause FD_WRITE and FD_READ events to be signalled. Each time an event is signalled on the socket it may also indicate the end of the handshake, which is checked each time as follows:

```
if ( SSLStatus == CONNECTING )
{
    int Result = SSL_connect( pSSL );
    if ( Result < 0 )
    {
        // Handshake not finished, or an error
    }
    else
    {
        SSLStatus = CONNECTED;
```

When the SSL_connect() call returns a positive value the handshake has ended successfully and the status of the channel is updated to CONNECTED. The example then prints some information of the peer's certificate and sends the GET request string to the server:

```
        int BytesDone = SSL_write( pSSL, pGetRequest, strlen( pGetRequest ) );
        if ( BytesDone < 0 )
        {
            // Most likely an error
        }
    }
```

This early in the connection there will be plenty of space in the socket's internal buffer, so there should be in theory no SSL_ERROR_WANT_READ or SSL_ERROR_WANT_WRITE results yet. Any negative result will likely be a real error in this case, but non-trivial programs should always check the value from SSL_get_error().

Receiving data

When data is received on the socket the FD_READ event is signalled. Each time this event is signalled the SSL_read() function is called to read any data that may be ready. It is possible that not enough data has yet been received by the TLS layer to be able to decrypt it. If this is the case then the SSL_read() function will return a negative value and a call to the example's HasSSLError() function is used to determine if it was an actual error or not.

```
if ( EventMask & FD_READ )
{
    if ( SSLStatus == CONNECTED )
    {
        char Buffer[ 2048 ];
        int BytesDone = SSL_read( pSSL, Buffer, 2047 );
        if ( BytesDone < 0 )
        {
            if ( HasSSLError( pSSL, BytesDone, "SSL: Unable to read!" ) )
            {
                return -1;
            }
        }
    }
}
```

Cleaning up

After the server has sent all its data it will terminate the secure channel and close the network connection. The example is notified of that by the socket signalling the FD_CLOSE event. At this point not all data may yet have been read from the internal buffer, which is something that needs to be done before closing the socket. The example reads all data from the SSL library by calling its ReadLastData() function and then return -1 to the main loop to signal that the connection closed.

```
if ( EventMask & FD_CLOSE )
{
    ReadLastData( pSSL );
    return -1;
}
```

The ReadLastData() function is pretty much the same as the one used by the TCP-Connect example, but with the socket's recv() function replaced by the SSL library's SSL_read().

There is no need to call the SSL_shutdown() function in this case since the network connection has already been closed. Nothing can be sent to the server any more, including shutdown handshake packets.

The SSL-Server example

This example is based on the TCP-Server example but uses a blocking socket instead. It still uses the asynchronous socket events. Since the asynchronous events are tied to the socket and not the SSL library it is possible that some events are signalled due to socket activity caused by the TLS part of the connection. This will then lead to SSL library functions being called, which will then block in order to perform TLS communication. For a CLI/Shell program this is fine since a user can always issue a Ctrl+C break to stop the program.

The example listens for connections on port 443, the standard port for a secure web server, it receives whatever the client sends and sends a string back to the connected client and then ends the connection. It uses a certificate and private key that are stored in the same directory as the example.

Preparing the library

The SSL library uses a context object to store its main state. This example will act as a server and creates a new context object intended for use by servers.

```
SSL_CTX * pCtx = SSL_CTX_new( TLS_server_method() );
if ( !pCtx )
{
    // This is an error, gracefully terminate.
}
```

A server requires a certificate as well as a private key to be used for the connection. The example uses the context object to load these. The certificate is done first so that the library can use the certificate to check the private key when that is loaded next.

```
if ( SSL_CTX_use_certificate_file( pCtx, pCert, SSL_FILETYPE_PEM ) != 1 )
{
    // This is an error, gracefully terminate.
}

if ( SSL_CTX_use_PrivateKey_file( pCtx, pKey, SSL_FILETYPE_PEM ) != 1 )
{
    // This is an error, gracefully terminate.
}
```

In the example folder will be a self-signed certificate as well as its matching private key. However, the AmiSSL library installation also contains a port of the openssl command, which can be used to create new keys and certificates. To create a key and matching certificate as files in PEM format the following command can be issued from the CLI/Shell. The openssl command can be found in the SSL: folder.

```
openssl req -x509 -newkey rsa:2048 -sha256 -days 3650 -nodes -keyout my.key -out my.cert
```

Accepting connections

When an incoming connection is received by the main socket the FD_ACCEPT event is signalled. Just like with the TCP-Server example, the new connection is then accepted by calling the accept() socket function, but only if no other connection is already active. When the connection is successfully established the accept() function will return a socket descriptor for it.

At this point the SSL object for the connection is created and the new socket descriptor is associated with the SSL object by calling the SSL_set_fd() function. The SSL object is also setup to automatically renegotiate in the background, should this be necessary.

```
pSSL = SSL_new( pCtx );
if ( !pSSL )
{
    // This is an error, terminate gracefully.
}

SSL_set_fd( pSSL, NewSocket );
SSL_set_mode( pSSL, SSL_MODE_AUTO_RETRY );
```

After this the server part of the TLS handshake should be started so that the client and server can setup the secure connection. This is done by calling the SSL_accept() function. Since the example is using blocking sockets the SSL_accept() function will block until the secure channel has either been setup, or if the handshake has been terminated due to an error.

```
if ( SSL_accept( pSSL ) != 1 )
{
    // This is an error, check ERR_get_error() for more information
}
```

Now the secure channel on the new socket is ready to start the exchange of data with the client that has just connected.

The new socket will have inherited the FIOASYNC flag from the main socket, thus enabling asynchronous events. But no events will have been yet been selected. The setsockopt() function is called to select the required events.

```
ULONG Temp = FD_READ | FD_WRITE | FD_CLOSE | FD_ERROR;
setsockopt( NewSocket, SOL_SOCKET, SO_EVENTMASK, &Temp, sizeof(Temp) );
```

Data transfer

After successful conclusion of the handshake the client will send its GET request to the server. On the server this will cause an FD_READ event to be signalled. The example will use the SSL_read() function to read the data sent by the client.

```
char Buffer[ 1024 ];
int BytesRead = SSL_read( pSSL, Buffer, 1023 );
if ( BytesRead < 0 )
{
    // This is an error, check ERR_get_error() for more information
}
```

When data has been read the SSL_write() function is used to send a string back to the client.

```
char * pStr = "The data to be sent back to the connecting client\n\n";
int BytesDone = SSL_write( pSSL, pStr, strlen( pStr ) );
if ( BytesDone  < 0 )
{
    // This is an error, check ERR_get_error() for more information
}
```

Since this is all the data the server is going to send it will also directly start shutting down the encrypted part of the connection.

```
SSL_shutdown( pSSL );
```

Because of the blocking socket the shutdown process of the encrypted part of the connection will have ended when the function returns. Now that the secure channel has been closed down, the socket can be shutdown for sending as well.

```
shutdown( EventSocket, 1 );
```

Cleaning up

The client closes the connection after reading the last data coming from the server. This will then cause an FD_CLOSE event to be signalled on the server. The server will then free the SSL object that was created for this connection and close the connection's socket.

```
SSL_free( pSSL );
CloseSocket( NewSocket );
```

At this point the main socket will still be open and still be accepting new connections.

To stop the program the user needs to issue a break signal by pressing Ctrl+C in the CLI/Shell. The example will then terminate gracefully.

First it will check if the *NewSocket* connection socket is still open, which can be the case if the user issues the break signal while a client is connected. If this is the case then the example will also check if there is a matching SSL object that needs to be freed and proceed with freeing the object as well as closing the connection socket.

```
if ( NewSocket != -1 )
{
    if ( pSSL )
    {
        SSL_free( pSSL );
        pSSL = NULL;
    }

    CloseSocket( NewSocket );
    NewSocket = -1;
}
```

Since the example is being terminated it is not necessary to call shutdown(). The next step is closing the main socket so no more incoming connections will be accepted and freeing the context object of the SSL library.

```
CloseSocket( Socket );
SSL_CTX_free( pCtx );
```

Now that all sockets are closed and all objects are freed the AmiSSL library can be closed. Then the Exec signal is freed and the example exits.

10. AmiSSL in assembler

Although there are no official assembly header files, the AmiSSL libraries can still be accessed by software written in assembly. Since the assembly code will be calling the same functions as the C code there will be a lot of similarities between the two.

The 'lvo' directory in the examples archive contains a number of assembly header files. These files contain the Library Vector Offset, or LVO, for each of the functions in the SSL library. The amisslmaster_lib.i file contains the offsets for the functions of the amisslmaster.library. The amissl_lib.i and amisslext_lib.i files contain the offsets for the two library pointers that are obtained with the OpenAmiSSLTagList() function of the amisslmaster.library.

For brevity the code shown here has most of the error recovery removed, the full source in the download will have most of this implemented. There therefore will be small differences between the code here in the book and the source code in the download.

All these examples are meant to be run from the CLI/Shell and not from the Workbench. This allows the examples use the CLI/Shell window to output status.

Setting up

Apart from the setup required for the bsdsocket.library (as shown in a previous chapter) there is now additional setup required for the SSL library. The requested stack size has also been increased from 10240 bytes to 20480 bytes.

Opening the library

The amisslmaster.library is opened like any other library on the system. The library is then used to open the best suitable AmiSSL library version that is available on the system. It is quite possible that a system does not have AmiSSL installed, even if it does have a network stack. When AmiSSL is missing a graceful exit with a suitable error message is preferred.

```
           MOVE.L   4.W,a6                        ; a6 = ExecBase
           MOVEQ.L  #AMISSLMASTER_MIN_VERSION,d0  ; Minimal version to open
           LEA.L    AmiName(PC),a1                ; APTR library name
           JSR      _LVOOpenLibrary(a6)
           MOVE.L   d0,AmiBase                    ; Store library pointer
           BEQ.W    .NoSSL                        ; NULL? No AmiSSL installed.

AmiName:   DC.B     "amisslmaster.library",0
```

The pointer to the amisslmaster.library can now be used to call the OpenAmiSSLTags() function. This will open the actual SSL library and provide two pointers to it, AmiSSLBase and AmiSSLExtBase. At the same time the call is used to give the SSL library access to the bsdsocket.library pointer and to the *ErrNo* variable.

```
          MOVE.L   AmiBase(PC),a6              ; a6 = AmiBase
          MOVEQ.L  #35,d0                      ; ULONG API version
          LEA.L    .SSLTags(PC),a0            ; APTR Taglist
          MOVE.L   SockBase(PC),4(a0)         ; Place APTR in taglist
          JSR      _LVOOpenAmiSSLTagList(a6)
          TST.L    SSLBase                     ; Is there an SSLBase pointer?
          BEQ.B    .Error                      ; No? That is an error

.SSLTags  DC.L     AmiSSL_SocketBase,0
          DC.L     AmiSSL_UsesOpenSSLStructs,0
          DC.L     AmiSSL_GetAmiSSLBase,SSLBase
          DC.L     AmiSSL_GetAmiSSLExtBase,SSLExtBase
          DC.L     AmiSSL_ErrNoPtr,ErrNo
          DC.L     TAG_DONE
```

Closing the library

While the program was running the SSL library may have allocated quite a number of structures and caches in memory. These need to be freed by calling the CloseAmiSSL() function before the master library is closed.

```
          MOVE.L   AmiBase(PC),a6              ; a6 = AmiBase
          JSR      _LVOCloseAmiSSL(a6)
          MOVE.L   4.W,a6                       ; a6 = ExecBase
          MOVE.L   AmiBase(PC),a1
          JSR      _LVOCloseLibrary(a6)
```

Getting error code information

The functions of the SSL library may indicate that an error has occurred. When this happens the ERR_get_error() function of the SSL library can be used to get the code for the error. The ERR_error_string_n() function can then be used to convert this code into a human readable string to be shown to the user as follows:

```
          MOVE.L   SSLBase(PC),a6             ; a6 = SSLBase
          JSR      _LVOERR_get_error(a6)      ; Returns error code in D0
          MOVE.l   #250,d1                     ; ULONG buffer size
          LEA.L    Buffer,a0                   ; APTR buffer
          JSR      _LVOERR_error_string_n(a6) ; Place string in buffer
          LEA.L    Buffer,a0                   ; APTR buffer with string
          BSR.W    Print                       ; Print to console window
```

The SSL-Client example

This example is based on the TCP-Connect example but is using a blocking socket instead. It makes a connection to port 443, the standard port for a secure web server, and sends a simple GET request for the root page on the server. After this it will wait for the data that is being sent by the server and disconnect when everything has been received.

The example takes either the IP address or the hostname of the server to connect to as an argument.

Preparing the context

The SSL library uses a context object to store its main state. Since this example acts as a client it will create a new context object intended for use by clients. It first calls TLS_client_method() to get a pointer to the method, which is then passed on to SSL_CTX_new() to create the context.

```
MOVE.L   SSLBase(PC),a6              ; a6 = SSLBase
JSR      _LVOTLS_client_method(a6)
MOVEA.L  d0,a0                      ; APTR Method

JSR      _LVOSSL_CTX_new(a6)
MOVE.L   d0,CtxObj                  ; Store APTR to context object
BEQ.B    .Error                     ; No object = error.
```

The context object is then used to setup the verification of the certificate that will be sent by the server during the initiation handshake. The function SSL_CTX_set_default_verify_paths() is called to make the SSL library use the default locations when looking for the root certificates on the system. Without this call the library will not look anywhere and only use certificates that were loaded by the example itself (which is none in this case).

```
MOVE.L   CtxObj(PC),a0              ; APTR Context object
JSR      _LVOSSL_CTX_set_default_verify_paths(a6)
```

Then a call to SSL_CTX_set_verify() is made to specify how the library should verify the certificate from the server. The call also provides a pointer to the verification callback function. This function will be called after the library has done its verification on a certificate and can be used to overrule the result of the verification.

```
MOVE.L   CtxObj(PC),a0                  ; APTR Context object
MOVEQ.L  #SSL_VERIFY_PEER|SSL_VERIFY_FAIL_IF_NO_PEER_CERT,d0
LEA.L    VerifyCB(PC),a1               ; APTR callback function
JSR      _LVOSSL_CTX_set_verify(a6)
```

The callback function itself will be shown later in its own section.

For each connection a separate SSL object is required. This object is created with the SSL_new() function, which takes the context object as an argument. After that the newly created SSL object is used to setup parameters for the upcoming connection.

```
MOVE.L   CtxObj(PC),a0              ; APTR Context object
JSR      _LVOSSL_new(a6)
MOVE.L   d0,SSLObj                  ; Store SSL object
BEQ.B    .Error                     ; No object = error
```

The example will use a SOCK_STREAM type socket to connect to the server and after that the SSL library will be used for the TLS parts of the connection. To be able to do this the SSL library will need access to the socket that will be used. This is done with the SSL_set_fd() function that takes the socket descriptor as its argument.

```
MOVE.L   SSLObj(PC),a0              ; APTR SSL object
MOVE.L   Socket(PC),d0              ; Socket descriptor
JSR      _LVOSSL_set_fd(a6)
```

The C example used the SSL_set_tlsext_host_name() macro to set the hostname of the server it is going to connect to. This is important when connecting to a server that hosts multiple sites as it informs the server which site's certificate is being requested. This macro is not available for assembly programs. It actually calls the SSL_ctrl() function directly, which is something an assembly program can do as well. The return value of the SSL_ctrl() function will be the same as it was for the SSL_set_tlsext_host_name() macro.

```
MOVEQ.L  #SSL_CTRL_SET_TLSEXT_HOSTNAME,d0   ; LONG cmd
MOVEQ.L  #TLSEXT_NAMETYPE_host_name,d1      ; LONG larg
MOVE.L   SSLObj(PC),a0                      ; APTR SSL object
LEA.L    HostName,a1                        ; APTR parg
JSR      _LVOSSL_ctrl(a6)
```

Similarly, the C example called the SSL_set_mode() macro to enable the auto retry mode. This ensures that any renegotiation during the connection will happen in the background.

Just like the previous macro, this macro is not available for assembly programs either. This macro also calls the SSL_ctrl() function directly and so the example again calls the SSL_ctrl() function with arguments that match the ones from the SSL_set_mode() macro.

```
MOVEQ.L  #SSL_CTRL_MODE,d0          ; LONG cmd
MOVEQ.L  #SSL_MODE_AUTO_RETRY,d1    ; LONG larg
MOVE.L   SSLObj(PC),a0              ; APTR SSL object
SUB.L    a1,a1                      ; APTR parg (NULL)
JSR      _LVOSSL_ctrl(a6)
```

The return value of the SSL_ctrl() function will be the same as it was for the SSL_set_mode() macro.

The handshake

The example uses blocking sockets, which means that the socket is connected to the server as soon as the connect() function returns with a success result. The handshake process is started with a call to the SSL_connect() function. Due to the blocking socket this function will only return when the handshake has either successfully finished or has been terminated with an error.

```
MOVE.L   SSLBase(PC),a6            ; a6 = SSLBase
MOVE.L   SSLObj(PC),a0             ; APTR SSL object
JSR      _LVOSSL_connect(a6)
CMPI.L   #1,d0                     ; Check result
BEQ.B    .HandshakeOK              ; One = all is well
```

The validation callback

While the handshake is being performed (and the SSL_connect() function is blocking) the server will send its certificate chain. The certificates in the chain will each be validated in turn and after each of these validations the callback function is called.

The arguments for the callback function are stored on the stack as 32 bits values. The first argument is named *pre_verify* and contains a boolean with the result of the verification process where a value of 0 means that the verification failed. The second argument is a pointer to the CTXStore object which can be used to obtain information regarding the current certificate.

```
VerifyCB:      MOVEM.L  a0/a1/a6,-(a7)            ; Store 3 registers on stack
               MOVE.L   SSLBase(PC),a6            ; a6 = SSLBase
               MOVE.L   5*4(sp),a0                ; APTR CTXStore object
               MOVE.L   4*4(sp),d0                ; LONG pre_verify
               BEQ.B    .Failed                   ; Failed when pre_verify is 0
```

If the verification failed then the example will call X509_STORE_CTX_get_error() to get the reason for the failure. The result is then checked to see if the certificate is self-signed. If that is the case then a warning is printed, but the certificate is allowed. Otherwise it will get a human readable error string from X509_verify_cert_error_string() and print it.

```
.Failed        JSR      _LVOX509_STORE_CTX_get_error(a6)        ; Place error code in D0
               CMPI.L   #X509_V_ERR_DEPTH_ZERO_SELF_SIGNED_CERT,d0
               BNE.B    .ShowError                              ; Not self-signed?
               ...
.ShowError     JSR      _LVOX509_verify_cert_error_string(a6)  ; Convert code into string
```

The callback function returns the result of its validation in register D0. When the return value is set to 0 then the validation has failed. This will terminate the handshake and the SSL_connect() function will return indicating a failure. When the return value is set to 1 then the validation was successful and the SSL_connect() function will return indicating a successful handshake.

Printing certificate information

It is possible to print information about the certificate that is being validated directly from the validation callback. This is done by calling X509_STORE_CTX_get_current_cert() with the pointer to the CTXStore object in register A0. The function will return with a pointer to the current certificate's X509 object in D0.

```
JSR       _LVOX509_STORE_CTX_get_current_cert(a6)
MOVE.L    d0,a0                    ; APTR X509 object
BSR.W     PrintCert
```

It is also possible to print the certificate information after the secure connection has been setup. This is done by calling SSL_get1_peer_certificate() with the pointer to the SSL object in register A0. This function will also return with a pointer to an X509 object in D0, unless the server did not send a certificate, in which case the function will return NULL. Depending on the type of program the server not sending a certificate may be a security issue and a reason for the program to disconnect with a suitable warning to the user. In the case of this example the printing of the certificate is skipped, but the connection is otherwise continued.

```
MOVE.L    SSLObj(PC),a0            ; APTR SSL object
JSR       _LVOSSL_get1_peer_certificate(a6)
TST.L     d0                       ; Was a cert sent?
BEQ.B     .NoCert                  ; No. Nothing to print
MOVEA.L   d0,a0                    ; APTR X509 object
BSR.W     PrintCert
```

The PrintCert routine expects a pointer to an X509 object in A0. It will use this pointer in a call to the X509_get_subject_name() function to get the certificate's subject and after that it will use X509_NAME_oneline() to convert the subject into a single printable line.

```
JSR       _LVOX509_get_subject_name(a6)
MOVEA.L   d0,a0                    ; APTR result
LEA.L     CertString,a1            ; APTR buffer for string
MOVE.L    #255,d0                  ; ULONG buffer size
JSR       _LVOX509_NAME_oneline(a6)
```

It then does the same for the certificate's issuer by calling X509_get_issuer_name() and converting this to a single printable line in the same manner.

```
MOVE.L    a5,a0                    ; APTR X509 object
JSR       _LVOX509_get_issuer_name(a6)
MOVEA.L   d0,a0                    ; APTR result
LEA.L     CertString,a1            ; APTR buffer for string
MOVE.L    #255,d0                  ; ULONG buffer size
JSR       _LVOX509_NAME_oneline(a6)
```

Data transfer

The secure channel with the server has been setup now that the handshake has finished successfully. All data being sent and received will be fully encrypted so that it cannot be peeked at by a 3rd party. Instead of the send() function of the socket library all data now needs to be transmitted with the SSL_write() function of the SSL library.

Before it sends the GET request the example will count the length of the string, excluding the byte taken by the terminator.

```
            LEA.L    GetRequest,a0        ; APTR Get request
            MOVEQ.L  #0,d0                ; D0 = Length counter
.Count      TST.B    (a0)+                ; Null-terminator?
            BEQ.B    .Done                ; Yes. Done counting
            ADDQ.L   #1,d0                ; Counted another char
            BRA.B    .Count               ; Keep counting
```

The simple GET request is sent to the server as follows:

```
.Done       MOVE.L   SSLObj(PC),a0        ; APTR SSL object
            LEA.L    GetRequest,a1        ; APTR Get request
            MOVE.L   SSLBase(PC),a6       ; a6 = SSLBase
            JSR      _LVOSSL_write(a6)
```

Similarly the data that is being returned by the server is not read with the socket library's recv() function but with the SSL library's SSL_read() function instead.

The example continues to call SSL_read() in a loop until a negative value or a value of 0 is returned. A negative value indicates an error, which will be printed to the console, while a return value of 0 indicates that the server has started the SSL shutdown handshake or it has already closed the connection.

```
.ReadAgain  MOVE.L   #2047,d0             ; LONG buffer length
            MOVE.L   SSLObj(PC),a0        ; APTR SSL object
            LEA.L    Buffer,a1            ; APTR buffer
            MOVE.L   SSLBase(PC),a6       ; a6 = SSLBase
            JSR      _LVOSSL_read(a6)
            MOVE.L   d0,.RdData           ; Copy result for printing
            BEQ.B    .NoConn              ; Zero? Connection gone!
            BMI.W    PrintSSLErr          ; Negative? That's an error.

            LEA.L    .RdStr(PC),a0        ; APTR FormatString
            LEA.L    .RdData(PC),a1       ; APTR Data for the string
            BSR.W    Printf
            BRA.B    .ReadAgain           ; Keep reading
```

The function also prints the number of bytes received each time a positive value is returned.

Closing and cleaning up

After the transfer has finished the encrypted part of the connection can be shutdown. This is done
via a call to the SSL_shutdown() function. When the SSL_shutdown() function returns the secure
channel has been shutdown and it is safe to close the socket.

```
MOVE.L   SSLBase(PC),a6          ; a6 = SSLBase
MOVE.L   SSLObj(PC),a0           ; APTR SSL object
JSR      _LVOSSL_shutdown(a6)

MOVE.L   SockBase(PC),a6         ; a6 = SockBase
MOVE.L   Socket(PC),d0           ; Socket descriptor
JSR      _LVOCloseSocket(a6)
```

Two objects were created with the SSL library that both now need to be released before the SSL
library is closed. The first one is the SSL object and the second one is the context object. Each
object pointer is checked for NULL so that the clean up function can be called at any time before
closing the program.

```
          MOVE.L   SSLBase(PC),a6          ; a6 = SSLBase
          MOVE.L   SSLObj(PC),d0           ; Get SSL object
          BEQ.B    .NoSSL                  ; Got none? Skip!
          MOVEA.L  d0,a0                   ; APTR SSL object
          JSR      _LVOSSL_free(a6)

.NoSSL    MOVE.L   CtxObj(PC),d0           ; Get Ctx object
          BEQ.B    .NoCtx                  ; Got none? Skip!
          MOVEA.L  d0,a0                   ; APTR context object
          JSR      _LVOSSL_CTX_free(a6)
```

Now that these last two objects have been freed the SSL library and socket library can be closed
and the example can exit.

The SSL-Client-NB example

This example is similar to the previous example but uses a non-blocking socket instead. There are a
lot of similarities, like the setup of the SSL libraries and the creation and clean up of the context
and SSL objects. These have not been included in this section, which will concentrate on the parts
that are different.

The example makes a connection to port 443, the standard port for a secure web server, and sends a
simple GET request for the root page on the server. After this it will wait for the data that is being
sent by the server and disconnect when everything has been received.

The example takes either the IP address or the hostname of the server to connect to as an argument.

Connecting to the server

When the TCP socket has made its connection with the server an FD_CONNECT event will be signalled. At this point the non-encrypted part of the connection has been made and the handshake to setup the encrypted part can be started.

On a non-blocking socket this requires multiple calls to the SSL_connect() function; the first one to start the handshake and the subsequent ones to check if the handshake has finished. To keep track of the state of the encrypted part of the connection the *MyStatus* variable is used. When the example starts the variable is set to NONE. When the FD_CONNECT event is signalled the variable is changed to CONNECTING.

```
EventConnect:   MOVE.W  #CONNECTING,MyStatus       ; We're now connecting the TLS part
                RTS
```

After checking if any of the other event bits are set in the event mask the example will check the *MyStatus* variable and if it is set to CONNECTING it will call its CheckSSLStatus() function. This function will call the SSL_connect() function to ensure the handshake is started and checks the result to see if it has finished.

```
                MOVE.L  SSLObj(PC),a0             ; APTR SSL object
                JSR     _LVOSSL_connect(a6)
                CMPI.L  #1,d0                     ; Result of one means successful ended
                BNE.B   .CheckResult              ; Not one? Needs to be checked
                MOVE.W  #CONNECTED,MyStatus       ; One! Secure channel is now connected
```

When the result in D0 has a value of 1 then the handshake finished successfully. If a different value is returned then this could indicate that an error occurred. If this is so can be found out by calling SSL_get_error() and checking its return value. If that is either SSL_ERROR_WANT_READ or SSL_ERROR_WANT_WRITE then no error occurred and the handshake is still ongoing.

```
.CheckResult    MOVE.L  SSLObj(PC),a0             ; APTR SSL object
                JSR     _LVOSSL_get_error(a6)
                CMPI.L  #SSL_ERROR_WANT_READ,d0   ; Not done reading yet?
                BEQ.B   .AllOK                    ; Not a problem
                CMPI.L  #SSL_ERROR_WANT_WRITE,d0  ; Not done writing yet?
                BEQ.B   .AllOK                    ; Not a problem
```

If there indeed was an error then this will be printed to the console window and the function will return a negative value to inform the main loop to gracefully terminate. One reason for failing could for example be the callback rejecting the certificate offered by the server.

```
                BSR.W   PrintSSLErr               ; Print error.
                MOVEQ.L #-1,d0                    ; Signal problem
                RTS
```

When the SSL_connect() function returns a value of 1 the secure channel has been setup successfully. The example will print the name of the connection's cipher to the console.

```
MOVE.L   SSLObj(PC),a0                ; APTR SSL object
JSR      _LVOSSL_get_current_cipher(a6)
MOVEA.L  d0,a0                        ; APTR cipher object
JSR      _LVOSSL_CIPHER_get_name(a6)
MOVEA.L  d0,a0                        ; APTR human readable string
BSR.W    Print
```

After that the example will print the peer's certificate information to the console, using the same functions as the previous example.

Data transfer

Directly after printing the cipher and certificate information the GET request is sent to the server. This is done exactly the same way as in the previous example by counting the number of characters in the GET request and then calling SSL_write() to send the string to the server.

The client and the server perform the TLS handshake by exchanging TLS data over the socket connection. This will result in a number of FD_READ events being signalled while the TLS handshake is in progress. The data received by the socket is intended for the SSL library and calling SSL_read() will be premature if the secure channel has not yet been established. For this reason each time an FD_READ event is signalled the *MyStatus* variable is checked before calling the SSL_read() function.

```
         CMPI.W   #CONNECTED,MyStatus        ; Secure channel connected?
         BNE.W    .Done                      ; No? Nothing to do

         MOVE.L   SSLBase(PC),a6             ; a6 = SSLBase
         MOVE.L   #4095,d0                   ; LONG Buffer size
         MOVE.L   SSLObj(PC),a0             ; APTR SSL object
         LEA.L    Buffer,a1                  ; APTR Buffer
         JSR      _LVOSSL_read(a6)
         MOVE.L   d0,.FmtData                ; Copy result for printing
         BMI.B    .Negative                  ; Negative = possible error
         ...
.Done    RTS
```

The return value of SSL_read() is stored in the data stream of a format string so that the number of bytes received can be shown in the console. If the return value is negative then SSL_get_error() is called to check if a real error happened, or if it is one of the SSL_ERROR_WANT_ results due to the use of the non-blocking socket. If it happens to be an error then the error is printed to the console, otherwise it will be ignored.

Closing the connection

The server will close the connection after it has sent all the data. The client will know about this when the FD_CLOSE event is signalled. This may happen before the client has managed to read all the data from the internal buffers, so it is important that all remaining data is read from the internal buffers before closing the socket. However, it is possible that the connection was closed before the secure channel was established, in which case there will be nothing to read and reading the data can be skipped.

```
          CMPI.W  #CONNECTED,MyStatus    ; Secure channel connected?
          BNE.W   .Done                  ; Not connected, no data
          MOVE.L  #NONE,MyStatus         ; No longer connected
          ...
.Done     RTS
```

Just like the previous example the rest of the data is read by calling SSL_read() in a loop until a negative value or a value of 0 is returned. A negative value indicates an error, which will be printed to the console, while a return value of 0 indicates that all data has been read.

Now that all data has been read from the internal buffer it is safe to close the socket. There is no need to call SSL_shutdown() since the socket connection is already gone. The server will have initiated the SSL shutdown handshake and the SSL library will have already processed that in the background before the server disconnected.

The SSL-Server example

This example is based on the TCP-Server example but uses blocking sockets instead. It still uses the asynchronous socket events. Since the asynchronous events are tied to the socket and not the SSL library it is possible that events are signalled due to socket activity caused by the encrypted part of the connection. This will then lead to SSL functions being called, which may then block in order to perform SSL/TLS communication. For a CLI/Shell program like this example this blocking is not a problem since the user can always issue a Ctrl+C break to stop the program. As a matter of fact, for this example that is the only way to stop it.

The example listens for connections on port 443, the standard port for a secure web server, it receives whatever the client sends and then sends a hard-coded string back to the connected client. After that it will end the connection. It uses a certificate and a private key that are stored in the same directory as the example.

Preparing the context

The SSL library uses a context object to store its main state. Since this example acts as a server it will create a new context object intended for use by servers. It first calls TLS_server_method() to get a pointer to the method, which is then passed on to SSL_CTX_new() to create the context.

```
MOVE.L   SSLBase(PC),a6            ; a6 = SSLBase
JSR      _LVOTLS_server_method(a6)
MOVEA.L  d0,a0                     ; APTR Method
JSR      _LVOSSL_CTX_new(a6)
MOVE.L   d0,CtxObj                 ; Store APTR to context object
BEQ.B    .Error                    ; No object = error.
```

The server will also need a certificate and its matching private key. The example expects the certificate to be named "My.Cert". It needs to be in PEM format and it should be stored in the same directory as the example's executable.

```
MOVE.L   CtxObj(PC),a0             ; APTR Context object
LEA.L    .CertName(PC),a1          ; APTR File name
MOVEQ.L  #SSL_FILETYPE_PEM,d0      ; int file type
JSR      _LVOSSL_CTX_use_certificate_file(a6)
CMPI.L   #1,d0                     ; Success?
BNE.B    .Error                    ; No!
```

The private key is loaded after the certificate. This file should be named "My.Key" and also be in PEM format and the same location as the example's executable. Loading the key after the certificate allows the SSL library to check if the private key is indeed matching the certificate.

```
MOVE.L   CtxObj(PC),a0             ; APTR Context object
LEA.L    .KeyName(PC),a1           ; APTR File name
MOVEQ.L  #SSL_FILETYPE_PEM,d0      ; int file type
JSR      _LVOSSL_CTX_use_PrivateKey_file(a6)
CMPI.L   #1,d0                     ; Success?
BNE.B    .Error                    ; No!
```

If there are any errors then the error will be printed and the example will terminate.

Accepting connections

The socket is prepared for incoming connections by binding it to port 443 and calling listen() on it. After that the example will start the main loop, which will use Exec's Wait() function to put the process to sleep until a signal becomes active.

If this signal is SIGBREAKF_CTRL_C then the user issued a Ctrl+C in the CLI/Shell window and the example will perform a graceful exit.

If the signal is socket related then the example will call its ProcessSocket() function. This function will call the GetSocketEvents() socket library function to find out which events happened and on which socket since the last call to GetSocketEvents().

The socket library will signal an FD_ACCEPT event when it receives an incoming connection. The example will then call the accept() socket function to accept the new connection. The accept() function will return a new socket descriptor for this new connection. Since the example can only have one incoming connection at a time it will call CloseSocket() on this new socket if there already is an ongoing connection.

If there is not already a connection active then the new socket descriptor is stored in the *NewSocket* location and the required asynchronous events will be enabled on it. The example will also print the address details of the incoming connection.

The example will then create a new SSL object since one is required for every connection.

```
MOVE.L    SSLBase(PC),a6        ; a6 = SSL base
MOVE.L    CtxObj(PC),a0         ; APTR Context object
JSR       _LVOSSL_new(a6)
MOVE.L    d0,SSLObj             ; APTR SSL object
BEQ.B     .NoSSLErr             ; NULL? That's an error
```

The socket descriptor of the new connection is then associated with the SSL object. This is the descriptor that was returned by the accept() function, not the one used for listen().

```
MOVE.L    SSLObj(PC),a0         ; APTR SSL object
MOVE.L    NewSocket(PC),d0      ; Socket descriptor
JSR       _LVOSSL_set_fd(a6)
```

The client connecting to the example will have started the handshake. To make the example do the server part of the handshake the SSL_accept() function is called. Due to the blocking socket the function will block until the handshake either ends successfully or is terminated.

```
MOVE.L    SSLObj(PC),a0         ; APTR SSL object
JSR       _LVOSSL_accept(a6)
CMPI.L    #1,d0                 ; Successful?
BNE.B     .NoAccept             ; No! Clean up
RTS
```

A result of 1 for the SSL_accept() function means that the handshake was successful and that the secure channel is now present. Any other value means that there was a problem and that the secure channel could not be setup. If that happens then the example will terminate the incoming connection and print a suitable error to the CLI/Shell window. It will not terminate the main loop, nor will it close the listening socket and will still be ready to accept further incoming connections.

Transferring data

The socket will signal an FD_READ event when it receives incoming data. This could be data sent by the client over the secure channel, but it can also be data that is part of the TLS protocol background communication. In response to the FD_READ event the example will call SSL_read(). If there is data from the client then the function will return that in the buffer. Otherwise the function will block until the client does send data, it disconnects, or some error occurs.

```
MOVE.L   SSLBase(PC),a6           ; a6 = SSLBase
MOVE.L   #4095,d0                 ; LONG buffer length
MOVE.L   SSLObj(PC),a0            ; APTR SSL object
LEA.L    Buffer,a1                ; APTR buffer
JSR      _LVOSSL_read(a6)
MOVE.L   d0,.RdFmtData            ; Copy result for printing
BMI.B    .Negative                ; Negative? Maybe an error
BEQ.B    .Nothing                 ; Zero? No data received
```

If the result from SSL_read() was negative then there was an error, in which case the example will print out the error. If there was a positive result then the example received data from the client and it will print out the number of bytes received.

If the example did indeed receive data from the client then it will send data back to the client. In this case it is a simple hard-coded character string that is sent back. The result of the SSL_write() function is not checked for errors and only printed to the console as the number of bytes sent.

```
MOVEQ.L  #WriteDataLen,d0         ; LONG buffer length
MOVE.L   SSLObj(PC),a0            ; APTR SSL object
LEA.L    WriteData(PC),a1         ; APTR Data to send
JSR      _LVOSSL_write(a6)
MOVE.L   d0,.WrFmtData            ; Copy result for printing
```

```
WriteData       DC.B    "The data to be sent back to the connecting client",10
WriteDataLen = *-WriteData
```

Since the example will not be sending any more data it will immediately start the shutdown process on the secure channel by calling SSL_shutdown().

```
MOVE.L   SSLBase(PC),a6           ; a6 = SSLBase
MOVE.L   SSLObj(PC),a0            ; APTR SSL object
JSR      _LVOSSL_shutdown(a6)
```

Due to the blocking socket the SSL_shutdown() function will only return after the shutdown process has finished. When the FD_CLOSE event is signalled the example will proceed by closing the connection socket and freeing the SSL object. After that it is ready again to accept further incoming connections on the main socket.

To stop the example the user needs to issue a break signal by pressing Ctrl+C in the CLI/Shell. The example will then terminate gracefully.

Before terminating the example will check if the *NewSocket* connection socket is still open. This can be the case if the user issues the break signal while a client is connected. If the connection socket is indeed still open then it will be closed.

```
MOVE.L   NewSocket(PC),d0          ; Descriptor of connection socket
BMI.B    .Exit                     ; Negative = already closed
JSR      _LVOCloseSocket(a6)
```

Since the example is terminating there is no need to call shutdown() on the socket first.

When all sockets are closed a call to the example's CleanUpSSL() function is made. This function checks all objects and frees them if necessary and calls CloseAmiSSL() when done. After that the example frees the Exec signal and closes all libraries and exits.

A. Network in WinUAE

The WinUAE emulator (can be downloaded from www.winuae.net) is used by developers and end users alike. Apart from great emulation it can also provide network access to the emulated Amiga. This can be done in two different ways and this appendix will discuss them both.

Emulating the library

The first method is the simplest – it provides the emulated Amiga with a bsdsocket.library that provides access to the network of the Windows computer. Since this library is also the network stack there is no need to install additional software on the Amiga.

It is enabled by selecting the *Expansions* option from *Hardware* in the list on the left hand side of the WinUAE configuration window. Then near the bottom in the section *Miscellaneous Expansions* tick the *bsdsocket.library* option.

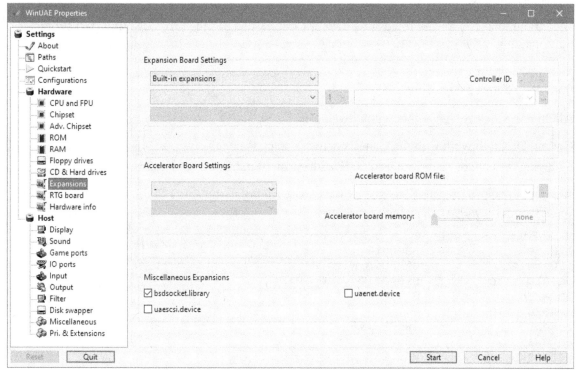

When the emulation is started the bsdsocket.library will be present in memory, available for network software to use.

Emulating a network device

WinUAE can also be used to emulate a network device. This option is enabled on the same configuration page as the library, but this time by selecting the *uaenet.device* option instead of the *bsdsocket.library* option.

When the emulation is started the Amiga will now have an uaenet.device in memory, which can be used by a network stack to access the network of the Windows computer. Since that requires additional software to be installed I don't usually recommend this to end users, but I do very much recommend this for developers. The main reason is that the emulated bsdsocket.library responds slightly differently than the bsdsocket.library of a native network stack like Roadshow or Genesis. The differences are small but could mean that software developed solely with the emulated bsdsocket.library does not work as expected on real hardware running a native network stack.

The emulated device provides network access using NAT and requires the network stack to use DHCP to get a valid IP address for the emulated network. Using DHCP is the easiest way to get this setup to work.

A configuration file for the Roadshow network stack (living in the DEVS:NetInterfaces directory) looks like this:

```
device=uaenet.device
configure=dhcp
```

All other options are left at their default values.

Getting DHCP to work with the Genesis network stack is not always possible, but this can be fixed by giving the network interface a static IP address of 10.0.2.15.

A configuration file for the Genesis network stack (living in the AmiTCP:db directory) that uses a static IP address looks like this:

```
INTERFACE
IfName              uaenet0
IfComment           GENESiS Wizard
Sana2Device         uaenet.device
Sana2Unit           0
Sana2Config
IPAddr              10.0.2.15
Gateway             10.0.2.2
Netmask             255.255.255.0
MTU                 1500
CarrierDetect       yes
NameServer          8.8.8.8
```

B. Glossary

Active connection – When two hosts are connected to each other the host that initiated the connection is said to have the active connection.

ASN.1 format – Abstract Syntax Notation One, a cross-platform language designed to describe data structures.

ARP – The Address Resolution Protocol is used by the IP protocol on Ethernet networks to find the MAC address of a system with a particular IP address.

Asymmetric cipher – A cryptographic algorithm that uses two different keys, one to be kept private and one that can be made public.

Asynchronous events – A system used by the bsdsocket.library to communicate changes in a socket's status (the events) to a running program.

Blocking – A blocking function will not return until something happens. This could be waiting for a connection or waiting for data to be transferred. This may mean that until the expected action occurs (or errors out) the application will seem to be non-responsive to the user.

Broadcasting – Sending out data that is not addressed to a specific host, but is sent to a special address so that all local hosts will receive it.

Brute forcing – Trying out all possible bit combinations of an encryption key until the one that decodes the encrypted data is found. The term is also used for trying out a large number of commonly used passwords to gain access to a system.

Certificate – A cryptographic object that contains identity information as well as a public key. The certificate is signed by a certificate authority and can be used to prove the identity of the certificate owner. The owner can be a person, a company or just a website for example.

Certificate Authority – A trusted institution that checks the identity information on a certificate before signing it.

Cipher – A cryptographic algorithm used for encrypting and decrypting information.

Datagram – The name used by the UDP protocol to refer to a single packet of data on the network.

DHCP – The Dynamic Host Configuration Protocol allows hosts to request a dynamic IP address from a DHCP server on the local network.

Dropping – When a packet is dropped it is removed from the sending queue without sending it further. The packet ceases to exist and the sending host may not be informed. The reason for this could be the TTL reaching zero or having the don't fragment flag set when fragmenting is required on the next link. It could also be security related or related to a lack of capacity on the next link.

Ephemeral port – When a socket is created and not bound to a particular port then a random port will be allocated. This random port is known as an ephemeral port since it will only be used for the duration of that socket. The next time the same application is used it is likely to be assigned a different port number.

Ethernet – A standard for physical networking. It describes connectors, wires and voltages and how data is transmitted across a single link.

Fragmenting – When a packet is too large to be sent over the next link then a router can break the packet up in multiple smaller parts called fragments.

Frame – The name used by the Ethernet protocol to refer to a single packet of data on the network.

Full-duplex – A type of connection where two hosts can send and transmit to each other at the same time without having to wait for each other. This allows both hosts to each use the full bandwidth provided by the connection at the same time.

Gateway – A host on an IP network that provides access to other networks like the Internet. The Internet router used by most home installations is normally acting as the local network's gateway.

Half-duplex – A type of connection where only one host can transmit at a time. For two hosts to have a conversation each needs to wait for the other to finish transmitting before transmitting themselves. This means that both hosts have to share the bandwidth of the connection.

Hash – A large number (usually 128 bits or more) calculated from data, like for example the contents of a file. If the data has been modified then this large number will have changed. Within cryptography this is used to verify that data has not been tampered with.

Host – Each system that has an IP address and is connected to an IP network is called a host.

Host identifier – The part of the IP address that is unique for each host on the network. It is the right-hand side of the address and marked by the '0' bits in the netmask.

Host order – There are several ways a number that consists of multiple bytes can interpreted. The order in which the host interprets them depends on the type of processor used. For the 680x0 family of processors this is most significant bit first, also known as 'little-endian' and this is the same order as used by the IP network.

HTTP – Hypertext Transfer Protocol, a protocol that sits on top of TCP and is used for retrieving data from web servers.

Key exchange – A secure method by which two parties can communicate (exchange) encryption keys with each other.

MTU – Maximum Transmission Unit, the size of the largest packet the network can handle. Different network links can have different MTUs and when a packet needs to traverse multiple links it is the link with the smallest MTU that limits the size of the packets used.

Multicasting – A method of transmitting data where multiple hosts will be able to receive the data. To receive the data each receiving host will need to join the multicast group the data is sent to.

Netmask – The netmask indicates which bits of the IP address are unique to the host (the host identifier) and which bits are used by all hosts on the local network (the network prefix).

Network order – There are several ways a number that consists of multiple bytes can interpreted. The order in which the network expects them is called the network order. For IP networks the network order is most significant bit first.

Network prefix – The part of the IP address that is the same for all hosts on the local network. It is the left-hand side of the address and marked by the '1' bits in the netmask.

Non-blocking – A non-blocking function will immediately return after calling. Since this does not indicate if the intended action has actually happened additional functionality needs to be used by the application to check the state of the action. On the Amiga the most efficient way of doing this is via the asynchronous events system.

Passive connection – When two hosts are connected to each other the host that received the connection is said to have the passive connection.

PEM format – Private Enhanced Mail format, which was originally intended to be used for securing email. It has been replaced by other secure mail protocols, but the file format for storing certificates and keys is still used.

Router – A system that is a node between multiple networks and decides for each packet over which network it will be sent. An example of the simplest setup is a router with only two networks, like an Internet router for home and office. A more complex router may have access to multiple networks and multiple possible routes to the same destination.

Secure channel – The encrypted part of the TLS connection.

Segment – The name used by the TCP protocol to refer to a single packet of data on the network.

Self signed – A certificate that has not been signed by a certificate authority. While the certificate may be valid, it is not possible to use it to prove the identity of the owner. As such it can be used to encrypt and decrypt the secure channel but the owner of the certificate may not be who they say they are.

Sigbreak – A sigbreak is used when a user tries to stop a program that is running in the CLI or Shell. The default key combination to send a sigbreak to a program is Ctrl+C.

Signal – A method used by AmigaOS to communicate that something is ready. A process/task can be put to sleep waiting for a number of signals and be woken up automatically when one (or more) of the signals becomes active. This is done in a multitasking friendly way so that a sleeping program does not take any CPU power from the other programs running on the system.

Signing – Calculating a hash over digital information and encrypting this hash with a private key. This then proves that the information has not been tampered with (as the decrypted hash won't match the information's hash when tampered with) and it proves the origin of the digital information (the public key of the signer of the information decrypts the hash correctly).

SSL – Secure Socket Layer, a standard of creating encrypted TCP connections over IP networks. Replaced by the TLS standard.

Station – Each system on an Ethernet network is called a station.

Symmetric cipher – A cryptographic algorithm that uses the same key for encryption as well as decryption.

TLS – Transport Layer Security, the current standard for creating various types of encrypted connections over networks.

TTL – The time-to-live counter in an IP packet. Each time the packet passes a router the TTL will be decremented before it is passed on to the next router. When it reaches zero then the packet will be dropped and is not passed on. This is done to limit the distance each packet can travel.

X.509 – The format in which TLS certificates are stored and transferred.

Also available…

ISBN: 9781690195153

The Commodore Amiga is known for the great capabilities it introduced at the time of its launch. These capabilities were down to the hardware as well as its graphical pre-emptive multitasking operating system, now usually referred to as the classic AmigaOS. The beauty of the classic AmigaOS is that it provides most of the things one would expect of a modern graphical pre-emptive multitasking operating system, but at the same time the OS is lean enough for the programmer to understand what is going on under the hood.

This book provides an introduction into the programming of the classic AmigaOS using C as well as assembly language. It is aimed at programmers who have not programmed for the Amiga before as well as programmers who did this years ago and would like a refresher before diving back in. A general knowledge of computer programming is therefore assumed. The first chapters provide information on setting up programming software on a classic Amiga. The chapter about the 68000 processor will provide an overview of the processor's inner workings and instructions. The chapters about Exec, Intuition, GadTools, ASL, Graphics and Diskfont will explain the usage of these libraries and the functionality they provide. The use of files, directories as well as low-level disk access is detailed in the DOS and Trackdisk chapters.

And also…

Bare-Metal
Amiga
Programming

For OCS, ECS and AGA

E. Th. van den Oosterkamp

ISBN: 9798561103261

Programming the 'bare-metal' means writing software that directly interacts with a system's hardware without the use of an operating system. The main reason for doing this is to increase efficiency as well as providing functionality that may otherwise not directly be supported by the operating system. While the Amiga has a powerful multitasking OS, most games and demos go the bare-metal way. They are programmed in assembly language and bypass AmigaOS in order to communicate directly with the custom chips to bring special effects and smooth animations.

This book is about programming the Commodore Amiga hardware directly, bypassing AmigaOS. It covers all three chipset versions released by Commodore: OCS, ECS and AGA. Each of the sub systems has its own chapter that explains their workings and provides a number of examples. Amongst the subjects covered are the audio hardware, the Copper, the Blitter, sprites and playfields. This book also covers using the disk controller as well as interfacing with joysticks, paddles, mice and the keyboard.

An understanding of Motorola 680x0 assembly programming is required to get the best out of this book. Some knowledge of the workings of AmigaOS and the Workbench is useful but not necessarily required.

Index

www.ingramcontent.com/pod-product-compliance
Lightning Source LLC
LaVergne TN
LVHW062317060326
832902LV00013B/2277